SAN FRANCISCO GIANTS

RETURN TO THE PINNACLE

2012 WORLD SERIES CHAMPIONS

San Francisco Chronicle

The Voice of the West
A Hearst Newspaper

Frank J. Vega, Publisher
Mark Adkins, President
Ward H. Bushee, Editor and Executive Vice President
Al Saracevic, Sports Editor
Gerry Spratt, Deputy Sports Editor
Jake Leonard, Assistant Sports Editor
Frank Mina, Deputy Managing Editor, Presentation
Judy Walgren, Director of Photography
Pete Kiehart, Photo Editor
Bill Van Niekerken, Project Content Editor

WRITERS
Bruce Jenkins
Ann Killion
Steve Kroner
Scott Ostler
Henry Schulman
John Shea

PHOTOGRAPHY STAFF
Lacy Atkins
Susana Bates
Noah Berger
Paul Chinn
Beck Diefenbach
Luanne Dietz
Carlos Gonzalez
Liz Hafalia
Lance Iversen
Alvin Jornada
Mike Kepka
Stephen Lam
Michael Macor
Elly Oxman
Sarah Rice
John Storey
Matt Sumner
Lea Suzuki
Brant Ward
Russell Yip

KCI SPORTS PUBLISHING

Peter J. Clark, Publisher **Molly Voorheis,** Managing Editor
Katherine D. Grigsby, Book Design **Nicky Brillowski,** Cover Design

© 2012 San Francisco Chronicle. www.sfgate.com

All rights reserved. Except for use in a review, the reproduction or utilization of this work in any form or by any electronic, mechanical, or other means, now known or hereafter invented, including xerography, photocopying, and recording, and in any information storage and retrieval system, is forbidden without the written permission of the publisher.

San Francisco Giants: Return to the Pinnacle, 2012 World Series Champions
is a supplement of the San Francisco Chronicle.
Copyright 2012 by San Francisco Chronicle.
All rights reserved. Unauthorized reproduction and distribution prohibited.

ISBN: 978-0-9885458-0-9 (PB)
ISBN: 978-0-9885458-1-6 (HC)

Printed in the United States of America
KCI Sports Publishing   3340 Whiting Avenue, Suite 5   Stevens Point, WI 54481
Phone: 1-800-697-3756   Fax: 715-344-2668
www.kcisports.com

CONTENTS

Contents..3
Introduction..4
Spring Training...6

FLASHBACKS

    No Wilson, Now What...10
    3 More Hits Give Cabrera 50 in May...................................14
    Perfect Major-League History..16
    Zero Hour Shutout Streak is at 36 Inings...........................20
    Giants Brightest of Stars..22
    Posey on Fire Since All-Star Break....................................26

Giant Feature: Brandon Crawford.................................28

    Perfectly Timed Pence Homer Keys Comeback................32
    No Good in this Goodbye...34

Giant Feature: Buster Posey..38

    Pagan Steps Up in Time of Need......................................42
    Making a September Pitch..46
    Giant Step...48

Giant Feature: Sergio Romo..50

Giant Feature: Barry Zito..54

NATIONAL LEAGUE DIVISION SERIES...........................56

NATIONAL LEAGUE CHAMPIONSHIP SERIES..................76

WORLD SERIES..104

INTRODUCTION

It was a season that started under a shroud of doubt, but ended atop a cloud of celebration.

The San Francisco Giants weren't supposed to win the World Series in 2012. Two years removed from their astonishing championship in 2010, there were too many questions to answer at the beginning of the season. Too many holes in the team's fabric.

Bearded closer Brian Wilson, the emotional heart of the team, was lost a week into the season. Catcher Buster Posey, the team's most talented player, was coming off a dreadful injury that had many doubting his ability to return to his previous level of play. How would outfielder Melky Cabrera do as a replacement for the departed Carlos Beltran? Could Barry Zito deliver in the rotation?

It all looked questionable as the Giants lost four of their first five, all on the road. It all seemed uncertain.

But in the home opener, staff ace Matt Cain took the ball, beating the Pittsburgh Pirates 5-0 in a harbinger of things to come.

By late May, the Giants had fallen 7½ games behind the Dodgers in the National League West.

On June 13, Cain put the baseball world on notice by hurling the 22nd perfect game in major-league history. It was the first perfect game in the franchise's 130-year history.

By that time in the season, Cabrera had answered all the questions about him with his bat, carrying the team through the month of May with a team-record-tying 51 hits in a month. Posey answered all his doubters on the field and at the plate, earning a spot on the All-Star team next to Cabrera and third baseman Pablo Sandoval.

And it was at that All-Star Game, in Kansas City, that Cabrera and Sandoval starred, helping the National League secure home-field advantage for the far-off World Series. The Giants were 46-40 at the time, only a half game out of the division lead.

Four days later, with a win over the Houston Astros, the Giants assumed the division lead, a position they relinquished for only three days of the season's second half.

As the season moved through July and August, the Giants picked up momentum. They also picked up key acquisitions in outfielder Hunter Pence and infielder Marco Scutaro. Both would prove vital in the postseason to come.

The team also lost its top hitter. On Aug. 15, Cabrera was suspended for 50 games, having tested positive for excessive levels of testosterone. As the All-Star MVP, and one of the most feared hitters in the lineup, this was huge news for the team and all of baseball. It was a black eye for the team, too. As Posey put it at the time, "Ultimately, it was just a bad decision."

It was a decision that would have crippled most teams. The 2012 Giants thrived, instead. They finished August with an 18-11 record, then went 19-8 in September, securing the division crown and setting up a magical tour through the postseason, in which they would again overcome huge obstacles.

In the Division Series, the Giants fell behind the Cincinnati Reds, two game to none. An insurmountable lead? Nope. Led by the brilliance of a durable bullpen, including a rejuvenated Lincecum, the Giants won three straight and took the series.

In the National League Championship Series, the Giants again fell behind, three games to one against the St. Louis Cardinals. Led by Scutaro, pitcher Ryan Vogelsong and the remarkable Sandoval, San Francisco again lived to fight another series, advancing in a Game 7 for the ages, ending in a driving rainstorm.

Then it was on to the World Series against a Detroit Tigers team that had just swept the New York Yankees in the ALCS. Powered by a legendary three-homer game from Sandoval and more great pitching and defense than anyone could count, the Giants answered the call, sweeping the Tigers.

The story arc of the season is told in the pages of this book through the words of San Francisco Chronicle staff writers like Henry Schulman, John Shea, Scott Ostler and Bruce Jenkins, and the images of the Chronicle photo staff.

The unlikely champions had answered all the questions before them. The only thing left to do was book the parade route.

– Al Saracevic
San Francisco Chronicle Sports Editor

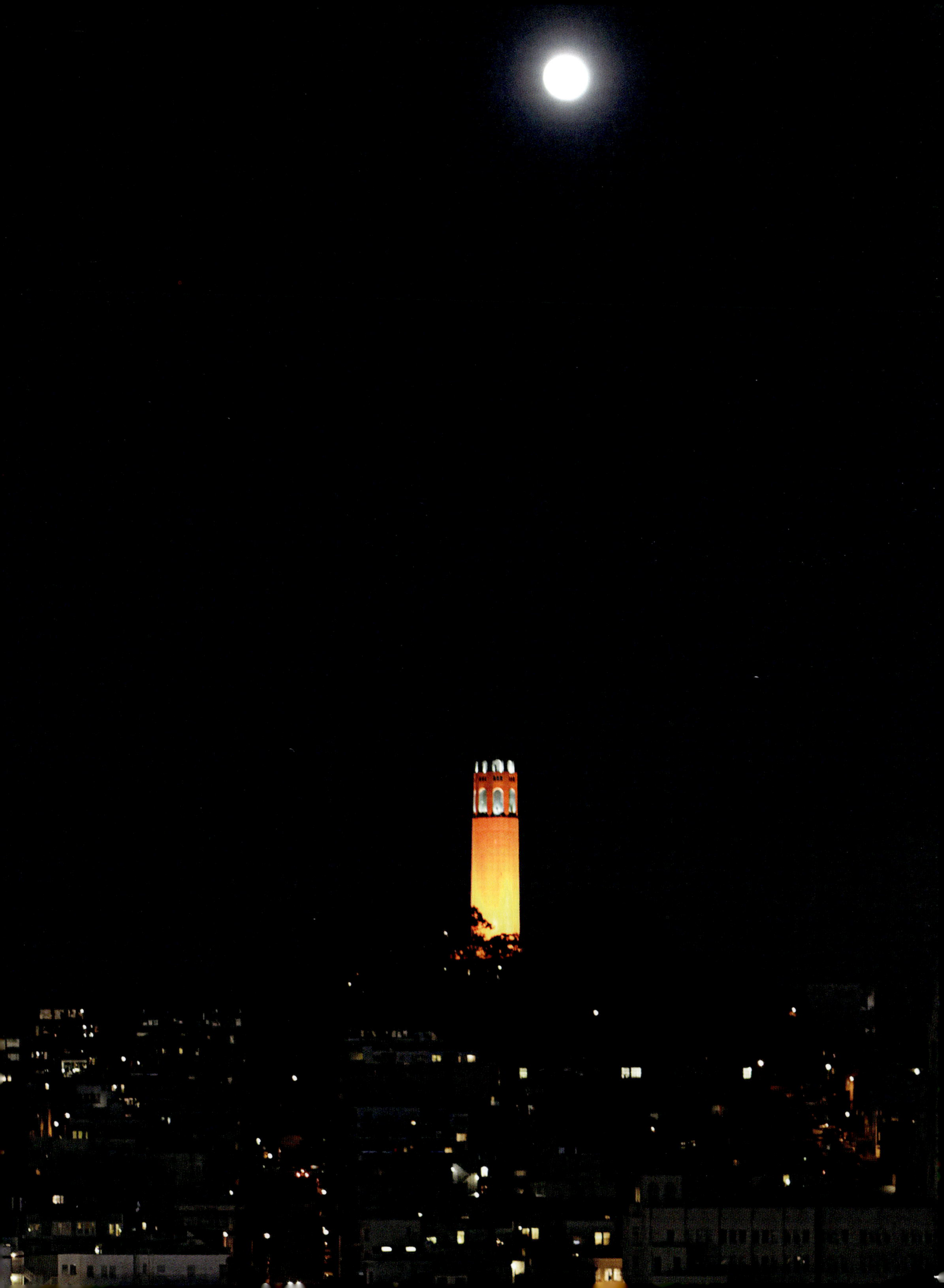

SPRING TRAINING

POSEY RETURNS
TO THE SCENE OF HIS PAIN

■ BY JOHN SHEA

Buster Posey has reached several post-injury milestones in spring training: First time running the bases. First Cactus League game. First at-bat. First hit (a home run). First time catching. First runner tossed out. First play at the plate. First slide into the plate. First time catching back-to-back games. First time catching Tim Lincecum.

Now comes the biggie, at least for Giants fans. First time playing in San Francisco.

The Bay Bridge Series begins Monday night, and Posey will play his first game at Third and King since May 25, the night Scott Cousins barreled into him in a home-plate collision that trashed the catcher's left ankle and sent him to an extensive rehab program that's still in progress.

More than 10 months later, Posey is feeling good about appearing at his home park again, saying of Giants fans, "They're a lot of fun to play in front of. We as players appreciate their passion and knowledge of the game."

The Giants are preparing for Friday's regular-season opener in Arizona. The A's already are 1-1 after splitting their season-opening series with Seattle in Tokyo and resume their regular-season schedule at the Coliseum on Friday, again against the Mariners.

In the Bay Bridge Series, the teams play again Tuesday night in Oakland and Wednesday afternoon in San Francisco. Posey will catch probably two of three.

"I'm optimistic because I thought I made a lot of progress this spring," Posey said. "I think it's only going to get better and better. I think the training staff has done a great job managing it, when to

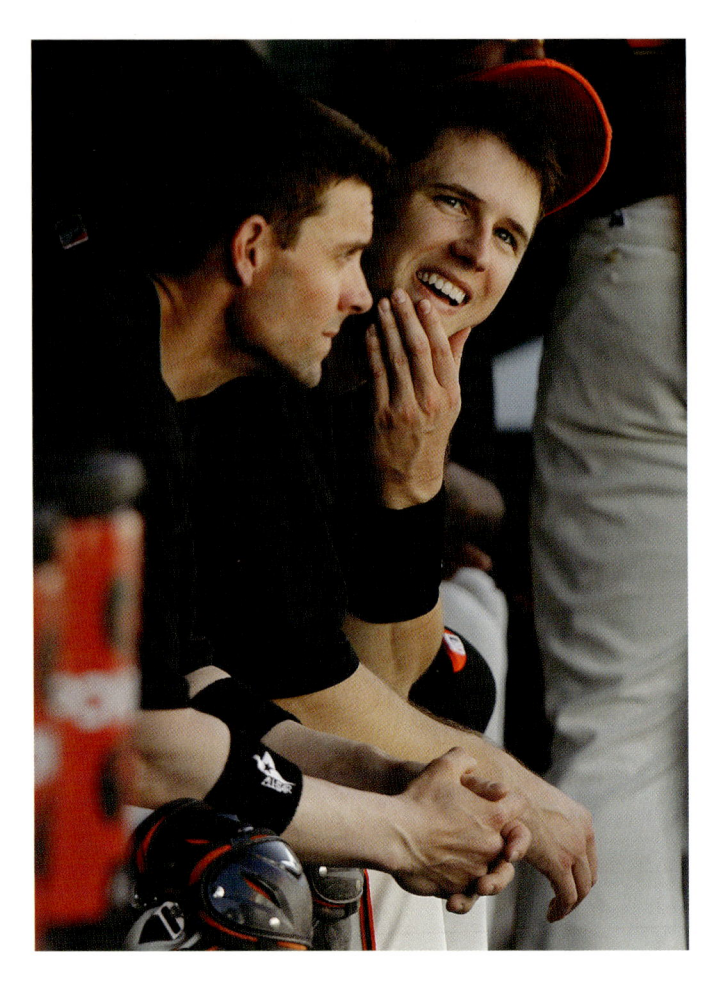

Above: Buster Posey sits with backup catcher Chris Stewart in the dugout during the San Francisco Giants' Cactus League spring training game. *Paul Chinn*

Following Page: Buster Posey made his return to the lineup in the San Francisco Giants' Cactus League spring training game. It was Posey's first game since his season-ending ankle injury last May. *Paul Chinn*

6   SAN FRANCISCO GIANTS: A RETURN TO THE PINNACLE

SPRING TRAINING 7

Above: Buster Posey loses his grip on the bat during a game against the Los Angeles Dodgers. *Lance Iversen*

push, when to hold back. I'm happy."

So are his teammates ...

"Now that he's come back and gotten to spend a full spring training with his team, he's back to being himself," Lincecum said. "It's one thing to know Buster's back. It's another thing to see him do what he did before he got injured."

Along with his manager ...

"We were optimistic he'd be fine," Bruce Bochy said. "We haven't had any hiccups with his rehab. (Trainer) Dave Groeschner did a terrific job with the rehab, and Buster came through all the stuff we put him through. I really think he's back to where he was."

With Sunday's 7-4 loss to the Brewers, the Giants finished the Arizona portion of spring training 16-14-3. The A's are 16-6-2, counting Arizona, two exhibitions in Japan and Saturday's 9-0 victory in Sacramento, in which they were still feeling the effects of jet lag.

"Sleeping, eating and back to sleeping again," second baseman Jemile Weeks said of his activities since returning from Tokyo on Thursday. Manager Bob Melvin called his nap on the team bus from the Coliseum to Sacramento's Raley Field "the best sleep I've gotten since I got back."

Graham Godfrey and Tyson Ross are starting the first two games of the Bay Bridge Series, hoping to nail down the final rotation jobs. Lefty Tommy Milone, who tossed six perfect innings on Saturday, was named the No. 3 starter behind Brandon McCarthy and Bartolo Colon.

Above: Catcher Buster Posey tries to throw out Miguel Cairo on a stolen base in the 2nd inning of the Giants Cactus League spring training. *Paul Chinn*

Cuban defector Yoenis Céspedes, who signed a four-year, $36 million contract, will make his Bay Area debut Monday and his Oakland debut Tuesday. He's 2-for-6 in the regular season with a home run and double. He batted seventh Saturday, as he did the first game in Japan, but ultimately is expected to be a 3-4-5 hitter.

For now, Weeks, Cliff Pennington and Coco Crisp are at the top of the lineup.

Asked to compare this year's offense with last year's, Weeks said, "It's an offense that wants to prove something, so you get more energy out of this lineup. Everybody's amped up to play, amped up to prove something. You've got a young team. Guys aren't very proven."

Melvin, a Giants catcher from 1986 to 1988, is familiar with the Bay Bridge Series as a player. This will be his first experience as a manager.

"I like the Bay Bridge Series," he said. "I know it's still spring training games, but if there ever was a series leading into a season where there's a little more weight than playing in Arizona, it's the Bay Bridge Series."

SPRING TRAINING 9

FLASHBACK

NO WILSON NOW WHAT?

■ BY BRUCE JENKINS

One game. That's how long the Giants were able to field a healthy, complete roster in front of their home fans. Game 2 at AT&T Park brought a crushing bit of news Saturday night, the likelihood that ace reliever Brian Wilson will be lost for the season due to elbow damage.

In light of what happened last year – losing Buster Posey in late May and never really recovering – it seems downright cruel.

There's a difference this time. If the Giants manage to stay in contention throughout the season, it will be because general manager Brian Sabean prepared for the worst over the winter. He made sure the Giants retained one of the deepest bullpens in baseball, and that could prove to be crucial as manager Bruce Bochy tries to offset a massive setback.

At a time when some felt he should focus on re-signing Carlos Beltran, Sabean sought other outfield options (Melky Cabrera and Angel Pagan) in the offseason while keeping left-handed relievers Javier Lopez and Jeremy Affeldt off the free-agent market. Affeldt is the man whose epic Game 6 performance helped the Giants win the 2010 NLCS against Philadelphia, and Lopez entered this season with a combined ERA of 2.38, allowing just 53 hits in 72 innings, since joining the team in July of 2010.

It seemed astounding that the highly valued Lopez wouldn't trigger a bidding war for his services, one that could leave the Giants out in the cold, but he didn't see the point of joining his sixth big-league team at the age of 34. "You know what it was? The high of 2010 lingered for me," he said

Above: Brian Wilson sits in the dugout during their game against the Arizona Diamondbacks at AT&T Park. *Ezra Shaw*

Following Page: San Francisco Giants pitcher Brian Wilson prepares to throw against the Oakland Athletics. The A's won 8-1. *Lance Iversen*

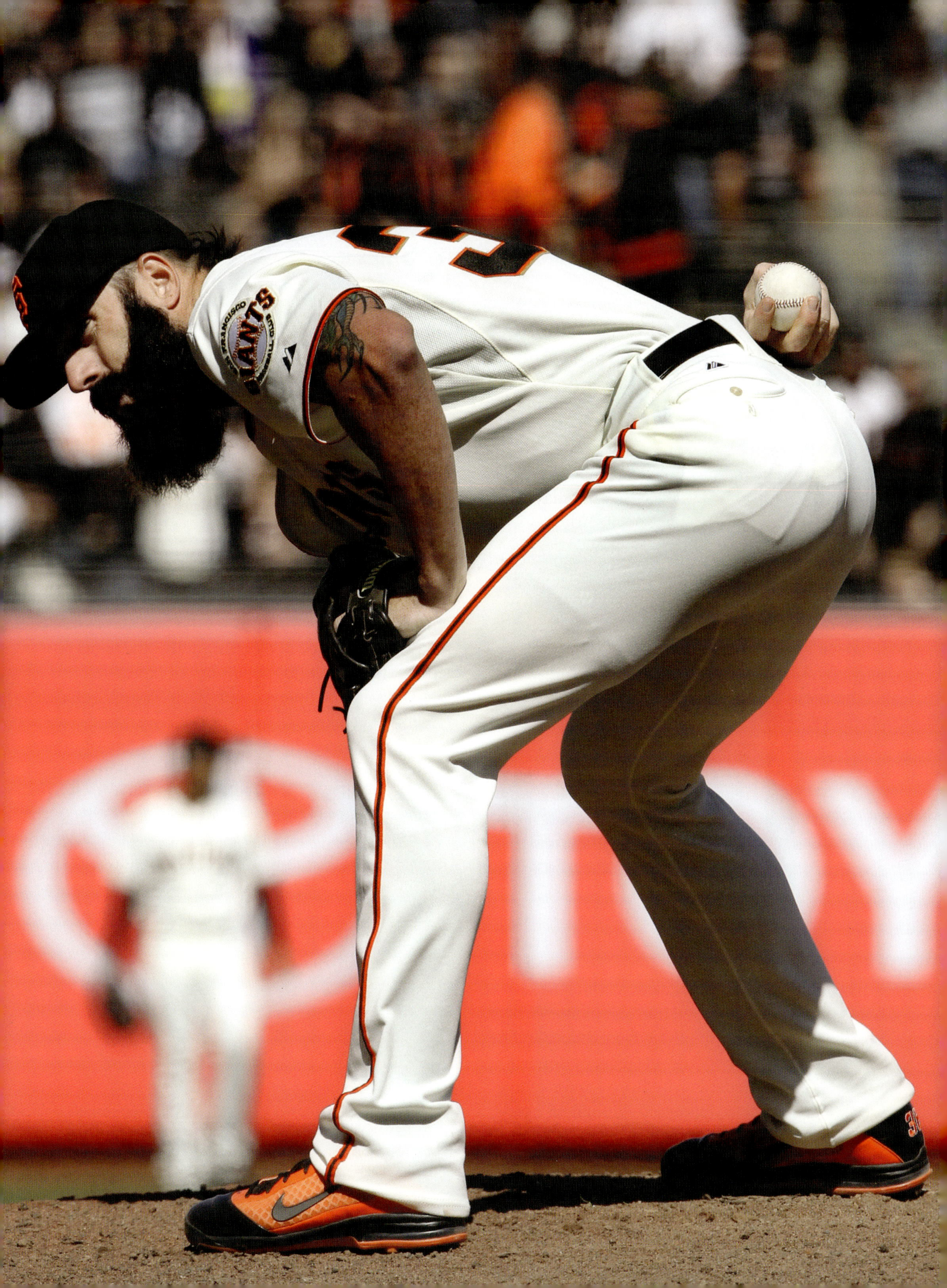
GIANTS

upon signing a two-year deal. "It doesn't hurt to play in front of a packed house, either."

Now Lopez becomes part of a closer committee, subject to Bochy's discretion each night, and for now, that group also includes right-handers Santiago Casilla and Sergio Romo, each of whom has elite stuff when he's on. Romo will be monitored closely, for he experienced mild elbow soreness this spring and missed some of his scheduled assignments.

"It's always nice to have one closer, but a committee works, too," Bochy said before Saturday night's game. "We've done that. We'll probably have to make slight adjustments as we go – who's available and who's not, those types of things. But we've got experienced guys who are comfortable pitching late in the game. This is certainly a tough loss for us, but the guys that we have could soften this loss – like the great job they did filling in last year when Willie was gone."

There was no immediate word as to whether Wilson would require surgery, but team sources believe it's a foregone conclusion. If so, it would be his second Tommy John operation (to repair ligament damage), dating back to 2003 when he pitched for LSU.

There was a time when such surgery ended a player's career, and even today, pitchers generally require at least one year to recover. The A's Brett Anderson had Tommy John surgery in July, and he is expected to return around that time this year. But another A's pitcher, Joey Devine, missed two full seasons (2009-10) after having the surgery, and Devine was recently placed on the disabled list with more problems in the elbow.

What it means, most likely, is that the Giants and their fans will be saying farewell to Wilson for a long, long time.

There's nobody to blame here, nothing to lament but the ferocious spirit of a true competitor. Wilson keeps himself in superb physical condition, and he has never been overworked – at least by conventional baseball standards – by Bochy and pitching coach Dave Righetti, renowned throughout baseball for keeping bullpens fresh and healthy.

Wilson has simply blown out his elbow, again, through the force of sheer desire. Much like Robb Nen, the sterling closer of the Giants' 2002 World Series team, Wilson never turns down a chance to finish a game, and he would never concede that he's injured in any way. Given that he wasn't quite himself last year and endured two stints on the disabled list, his problems probably stem from the 2010 stretch drive, when his tireless work shut down the opposition time after time – right through Game 5 of the World Series, when he struck out Nelson Cruz to clinch the Giants' first world title in San Francisco.

There were signs all spring that Wilson wasn't right, especially as he recorded a difficult save in his last outing (Thursday) in Colorado. Wilson called for trainer Dave Groeschner at one point during that 32-pitch appearance, ostensibly to check a turned ankle, "but that was no ankle injury," said a source close to the team. "You got the feeling his arm was killing him."

Now the Giants' attention turns to Fresno, where 6-foot-4 reliever Heath Hembree has begun his first season at the Triple-A level. Hembree didn't draw much notice in the 2010 draft - the Giants took him in the fifth round - but he has developed into a fearsome reliever with 95 to 98 mph velocity and increasingly sharp breaking pitches.

Bobby Evans, the Giants' vice president of baseball operations, said the Giants would prefer to leave Hembree at Fresno, where he has worked three shutout innings with two saves so far. That's the sensible call, Hembree having pitched only 64 1/3 innings of pro ball. If it reaches the point where Hembree is simply dominating the Pacific Coast League - with more command of his stuff than the Giants have witnessed to date - there's a chance he'll get a shot at the big leagues this season.

Following Page: San Francisco Giants relief pitcher Brian Wilson waves to the fans after warming up.
Lance Iversen

FLASHBACK 13

FLASHBACK

3 MORE HITS GIVE CABRERA 50 IN MAY

BY JOHN SHEA

Melky's May magic is almost over. Not because Melky Cabrera is going to stop hitting, but because he's running out of month.

The Giants' 3-1 victory over the Diamondbacks on Tuesday night had Cabrera's fingerprints all over it, which has become a theme. The left fielder added three more hits to the month of his life, including a record-breaking single in the decisive eighth-inning rally that prompted a standing ovation from the China Basin assembly.

Cabrera, gaining in popularity by the swing, lifted his helmet in appreciation.

On the Giants' bandwagon – or Melkwagon – Cabrera is front and center. His 50 hits in May set a San Francisco record, topping Willie Mays' 49 in May 1958. Cabrera is one hit shy of the San Francisco record for hits in any month (Randy Winn, September 2005).

"I've never seen anything like it," Ryan Theriot said.

Reminded he played in St. Louis with Albert Pujols, Theriot said, "He's got 50 hits in one month. That's impressive."

Cabrera said he was informed before the game by batting coach Hensley Meulens that he was closing in on the record, that three more hits would pass Mays.

"I wasn't aware of it," Cabrera said. "I'm very happy I was able to equal a record by Willie Mays, and maybe one day I can be like Willie Mays myself."

Above: San Francisco Giants outfielders Melky Cabrera, Gregor Blanco and Angel Pagan celebrate their 4-2 win over the Arizona Diamondbacks.
Lance Iversen

Above: Melky Cabrera broke Willie Mays' Giants record for hits in the month of May. *Sarah Rice*

Nothing like shooting for the top.

"Anytime you're in a category with Willie Mays, there's something to be said about that," said Ryan Vogelsong, who gave up one run in seven innings. "I'd like to see him get a couple more (Wednesday) and see him up there by himself."

After Theriot drew a walk to open the eighth, Cabrera collected his third hit, a single through the right side, and Buster Posey's sacrifice fly broke a 1-1 tie. With the bases loaded, Joaquin Arias hit a chopper and hustled to first base, avoiding a double play and pushing home another run.

Cabrera showed in his sixth-inning at-bat how truly blessed he is by the baseball gods, hitting a squibber down the third-base line that Josh Bell let roll, hoping it would spin foul. Of course, it rolled all the way past the bag in fair territory, and Cabrera was safe at first.

Posey doubled to left-center, scoring Cabrera to make it 1-1.

Cabrera's first hit, a liner to left with one out in the fourth, was the Giants' first off lefty Joe Saunders, who had much better success Tuesday than on May 13, when the Giants rocked him for six runs and 10 hits.

The Diamondbacks scored their only run on Bell's second-inning single.

Clay Hensley pitched a 1-2-3 eighth for the win. Santiago Casilla earned his 14th save with a perfect ninth.

The Giants are 5 1/2 games behind the Dodgers, the closest they've been to first place since May 10. For just the second time this season, the Giants have gained ground on the Dodgers in consecutive days, the first coming on April 17-18.

Unfortunately for Cabrera and the Giants, the final game of May is Wednesday.

"It doesn't seem like he's going to slow down," Theriot said of the majors' leader in hits (77) and multiple-hit games (25).

FLASHBACK 15

FLASHBACK

PERFECT
MAJOR-LEAGUE HISTORY

BY BRUCE JENKINS

The Giants' franchise has been playing baseball in the National League since 1883, going back to their New York days. They've won World Series, they've had no-hitters pitched, they've showcased the historic power of Barry Bonds and the all-around magnificence of Willie Mays. Never, in all those years, did they have a perfect game.

Matt Cain changed all that Wednesday night at AT&T Park, retiring all 27 batters he faced in the Giants' 10-0 victory over the Houston Astros. It came before a sellout crowd, and as Cain made his post-game remarks on KNBR radio, he marveled at the still-packed stadium.

"I don't think there's an empty seat right now," he said. "Unbelievable."

It was only the 22nd perfect game in major-league history and the 20th since the so-called "modern era" began in 1900. No-hitters have become relatively commonplace.

It is quite another story, however, to achieve perfection. There's no room for a walk, or an error or a hit batter. Each batter must be dispatched - no complications.

That's what made Cain's effort so special - and what undoubtedly caused such elation in the Giants' front office. This was the signature stroke of the Giants' modern-day identity.

The team takes a lot of heat for its inability to score runs, making for lively conversation on the daily talk shows. Never mind that it was pitching that carried the team to a world championship, its first in San Francisco, in 2010. The team fell badly short on the offensive end last year, and this year's team has hardly been an offensive juggernaut.

How fitting, then, that the team handed Cain 10 runs and all the comfort he needed.

And how appropriate, as the Giants solidify this new identity, that Cain signed a five-year extension to his contract, lasting through the 2017 season, in the first week of April.

Whenever a no-hitter or perfect game is pitched, there are defensive plays in the field that make it possible. The Giants got one of those plays Wednesday night from right fielder Gregor Blanco, and it will go down as one of the greatest, most timely plays in franchise history.

Jordan Schafer was leading off the seventh inning for the Astros, a light-hitting team in fifth place in the National League's Central Division. The count went to 3-and-2, meaning Cain had to throw a strike. He went with the fastball, Schaeffer hit a rocket to deep right-center and Blanco, after an all-out sprint, made a diving, one-handed catch.

As the stadium rocked with energy, Cain said he had to take a moment to calm himself down. "I literally felt everybody (in the crowd) on the mound with

Opposite Page: Giants pitcher Matt Cain celebrates after the final out against the Houston Astros in San Francisco. *AP Photo/Jeff Chiu*

SAN FRANCISCO GIANTS: A RETURN TO THE PINNACLE

FLASHBACK 17

me," he told KNBR. "The whole stadium. What a tremendous catch."

In an era in which nine-inning performances are rare, and pitchers tend to wear down after a long night, Cain seemed to be gathering steam. He was unleashing fastballs in the mid-90-mph range to the finish, always in harmony with his catcher, Buster Posey.

"Everything about the defense allowed me to go and pitch comfortably," he said. "I can't thank Buster enough. I never questioned him once. He was going to have me throw whatever he wanted, and I was gonna let him go."

Pitchers tend to be lousy hitters, but Cain is not among them - he is a ballplayer. Under such special circumstances, when it comes time to bat, many pitchers would be happy to go up there, watch three strikes go by and take a seat in the dugout. On the night of his life, Cain never stopped playing the game. He took a hefty cut at Xavier Cedeño's pitch in the bottom of the seventh, hustling down the first-base line as he grounded out to third.

That's what the fans love about Cain: his competitiveness, his humility, and the fact that he never, ever strays from character.

This was a night for Giants' fans to cherish exactly what they have these days: a likable, contending team and nightly sellouts at their China Basin stadium. Other clubs face attendance issues, even in good times - not here. Every night, from spring into autumn, is a happening at AT&T.

"It was just so exhilarating, sharing this with them," said Cain. "My emotions ... just unspeakable right now. I was locked in with that crowd all night."

On the night he made franchise history, the feeling was mutual.

18 SAN FRANCISCO GIANTS: A RETURN TO THE PINNACLE

Above: Giants' pitcher Matt Cain celebrates with teammates after throwing a perfect game against the Houston Astros at AT&T Park. Cain pitched the 22nd perfect game in major-league history and first for the Giants, striking out a career-high 14 to beat the Astros 10-0. *AP Photo/Jeff Chiu*

FLASHBACK

ZERO HOUR
SHUTOUT STREAK IS AT 36 INNINGS

■ BY STEVE KRONER

Nothing lasts forever. It only seems as if the Giants' pitchers' streak of nothing has lasted forever.

Actually, make it 36 scoreless innings and four consecutive shutouts after Madison Bumgarner one-hit Cincinnati in the Giants' 5-0 waltz at AT&T Park on Thursday night, which put the Giants in sole possession of first place for the first time in 2012.

In the 130 seasons of Giants baseball, this is the first time they have thrown four shutouts in a row.

"Amazing. It really is, " Giants manager Bruce Bochy said. "I've never seen it. ... It shows you how good these guys can be when they're locked in."

Bumgarner (10-4) was locked in to the tune of eight strikeouts and two walks in his first career complete game. Catcher Ryan Hanigan's single to center leading off the sixth was the only hit off the 22-year-old lefty.

The longest scoreless-innings streak in S.F. Giants history had been 35, spread over five games in May 1960 at Candlestick Park. The pitchers in that stretch: Billy O'Dell, Sam Jones, Jack Sanford and Mike McCormick.

After he pitched the top of the eighth, Bumgarner went into the Giants' clubhouse and saw that he and his teammates had just tied that 1960 mark.

His reaction: "Oh gosh, no pressure."

Left: Bruce Bochy congratulates Madison Bumgarner after the game against the Cincinnati Reds. Bumgarner pitches a one-hit shutout as the San Francisco Giants defeated the Cincinnati Reds 5-0.
Jason O. Watson/Getty Images

Opposite Page: Buster Posey slides into home for a run ahead of a tag by Johnny Cueto of the Cincinnati Reds.
Jason O. Watson/Getty Images

He handled that pressure with a 1-2-3 ninth, and then his teammates gave Bumgarner a shower of beer and shaving cream.

"Madison, he was in charge the whole way," Bochy said. "I actually thought he got a little better as the game went along, too."

Bumgarner went 5-0 in June. The Giants began the month with a four-game winning streak. They've matched that, which is their longest of the season. And with the Dodgers losing 3-2 to the Mets, the Giants climbed atop the NL West.

As for the offense, after Johnny Cueto (9-4) retired his first two hitters of the night, the Giants put together a two-run rally. A walk to Melky Cabrera preceded Buster Posey's single to right.

Angel Pagan followed Posey by pulling a base hit to right – and that set off a harried sequence. Right fielder Jay Bruce threw to the plate, though he didn't have much of a chance to nail Cabrera.

Not only did Cabrera score, but Bruce's throw short-hopped Hanigan and bounced toward the Reds' on-deck circle. Posey hustled home and beat Hanigan's throw to Cueto, who was covering.

Pagan tried to motor all the way to third, but Cueto fired the ball to Scott Rolen, whose tag on Pagan ended the sequence and the inning. The Giants were in front to stay.

Now it's Matt Cain's turn to try to keep the scoreless streak going. Cain, of course, pitched a perfect game against Houston on June 13. He'll face a little different chore Friday night against the Reds.

Bumgarner gave Cain some advice after Thursday's win.

Said Bumgarner: "I said, 'Don't worry about it. There's no pressure. All you've got to do is throw a shutout.'"

FLASHBACK 21

FLASHBACK

GIANTS
BRIGHTEST OF STARS

■ BY JOHN SHEA

The rest of the nation mocked, abused and laughed at Giants fans, calling them over-the-top homers for stuffing the ballot box and voting for anyone in orange and black, healthy or not.

The fans got it right.

"Thank you," Matt Cain said with a celebratory chuckle, the winning pitcher in the National League's 8-0 victory over the American League in Tuesday night's 83rd All-Star Game. "That couldn't have been any better. I appreciate that, especially on my end of it, to get that lead early with Panda hitting the triple.

"I can't thank the fans enough to be able to vote them in. That shows the support we have in the Bay Area."

Panda, a.k.a. Pablo Sandoval, who had zoomed past Mets third baseman David Wright in the final week of All-Star voting, hit a three-run triple to highlight a five-run first inning.

Melky Cabrera, who surged from fourth to first among outfielders late in the voting process, hit a homer and single and was named the game's MVP.

And Buster Posey, who received the NL's most votes (7.6 million), caught Cain's scoreless two innings and drew a first-inning walk. Cabrera, Posey and Sandoval all scored in the first inning.

"I'm happy fans made the right decision with all those guys," Sandoval said.

The decision to start Cain was NL manager Tony

Above: National League All-Star Melky Cabrera holds up the Ted Williams Most Valuable Player Award after the National League won 8-0.
Jonathan Daniel/Getty Images

Above: National League All-Star Melky Cabrera hits a two-run home run in the fourth inning during the 83rd MLB All-Star Game at Kauffman Stadium. *Jonathan Daniel/Getty Images*

La Russa's, much to the chagrin of R.A. Dickey and Mets fans, and that turned out OK, too. Cain retired six of seven batters, and only leadoff man Derek Jeter reached base on a single off Sandoval's glove.

The 5-0 first-inning lead, something about which Cain has known little, considering his history of minimal run support, stood the rest of the night. Cain and 10 other pitchers limited the AL to six hits, and the NL scored three more times in the fourth – a rally featuring Cabrera's two-run homer – to cotinue the party for Giants fans.

"I didn't come to win an MVP," Cabrera said. "That's just a surprise. It's a great gift the Lord gave me."

Hard-throwing AL starter Justin Verlander admitted his approach was backward. Usually, he saves his 100-mph fastballs for late innings, but he threw them right away this time.

"That's why I don't try to throw 100 in the first inning, " Verlander said." We're here for the fans. I know fans don't want me to throw 90 and hit the corners. They want to see the 100-mph fastball, so I gave them that."

It backfired. Posey's walk came on four pitches, filling the bases for Sandoval, who hit a curve high enough down the right-field line that the sun momentarily blocked Jose Bautista's vision. It was Sandoval's first triple of 2012 and the first bases-loaded triple in All-Star history.

"That's always fun, to watch Pablo run," Cain said.

"I never faced him before," Sandoval said of Ver-

FLASHBACK 23

Above: The San Francisco Giants' Pablo Sandoval watches the flight of his triple in the first inning in the MLB All-Star Game at Kauffman Stadium in Kansas City, Mo. *Rich Sugg/Kansas City Star/MCT*

lander, "and was just trying to put the ball in play. He didn't have control of his fastball. I got a pitch I could hit."

Cabrera opened the rally by hitting a one-out single and scoring on Ryan Braun's double, appearing as an orange blur around the bases in his new bright spikes. Sandoval also was decked out in orange shoes, an All-Star gift from his manufacturer.

Posey received a couple of pairs but chose not to wear them. He was all business and no flash in his first All-Star appearance. Cain had no choice. He didn't get a new pair.

"That would've been a little bit out of my realm, I think," Cain said.

Said Posey: "You guys know that's not quite my style."

Several NL players said a pregame speech by Chipper Jones, appearing in his final All-Star Game, was inspiring. It especially hit home for Posey, who followed the Braves' third baseman growing up in Georgia.

Posey said he was touched "regardless where I'm

from because of the type of career he's put together. He basically said go out there and leave everything you've got. Have some fun, but realize everyone's here for a reason."

Cain did all that.

"It almost felt like the adrenaline was more than what it was in the playoffs," Cain said, "because you know you're only going one or two innings and you're going to let it all hang out."

By winning, the NL owns the home-field advantage in the World Series, and the NL pennant winner will host the first two games.

"It was big for us to have those first two games in San Fran, " Posey said of the 2010 World Series." I don't think guys play the game any differently if it weren't for home-field advantage. We all have pride in what we do that we're going to play the game hard. But it definitely makes it more interesting for fans."

And as we know, the fans made it all possible.

Below: National League All-Star Matt Cain pitches in the first inning during the 83rd MLB All-Star Game. *Jonathan Daniel/Getty Images*

FLASHBACK

POSEY ON FIRE
SINCE ALL-STAR BREAK

BY HENRY SCHULMAN

Buster Posey and his peeps have put out a video game for Apple devices called "Buster Bash." It's a hit inside the Giants clubhouse. A bunch of guys were playing it before batting practice Tuesday.

"Why is it so addicting?" Aubrey Huff hollered.

As a team that still has not found offensive consistency after 110 games, the Giants are just as addicted to the real Posey. They need their nightly fix, and he provided one Tuesday night with an early swing that sent Barry Zito and the Giants to a 4-2 victory over the Cardinals.

Posey hit a three-run homer in the first inning off 13-game winner Lance Lynn, his 18th of the season, to match the career high he set as a rookie in 2010.

Zito and a newly arranged bullpen made it stand against the league's highest-scoring offense in the Giants' fourth win in five games on what will be a winning trip.

Posey is climbing the ladder in every major offensive category in the National League, enough to place him in the Most Valuable Player conversation even if he (or anyone else) is a longshot to overtake Pittsburgh's Andrew McCutchen.

"That's humbling to even be mentioned in something like that, " Posey said. "It's pretty cool, I guess."

When Posey won National League Player of the Month in July 2010, he hit .440 with

Above: Buster Posey hits a three-run home run during the fifth inning of the game against the San Diego Padres. *Beck Diefenbach*

six homers and 23 RBIs during a 21-game hitting streak.

He blew past those numbers in his first 21 games after the All-Star break this year, hitting .458 with seven homers and 27 RBIs.

That was through Monday. On Tuesday, he impacted Game 22 quickly after Angel Pagan and Marco Scutaro singled. Catcher Yadier Molina called for a slider well off the plate, but Lynn hit the outside corner and Posey sent the ball the other way into the bleachers in right-center field for a 3-0 Giants lead. That made it easier for Zito to be aggressive.

"In the first inning he looked crisp with all his pitches and command, " manager Bruce Bochy said. "He had a good look about him. I've had him for a while. You can see the difference when he's off or on."

Zito was coming off two bad outings and pitching in a park that has chewed him up. But he held the Cardinals to two solo homers by Allen Craig in 6 $\frac{2}{3}$ innings.

A bullpen that learned of a new world order in a pregame talk with Bochy and pitching coach Dave Righetti held St. Louis scoreless over the final 2 $\frac{1}{3}$ innings. Clay Hensley got one out, Sergio Romo two and Jeremy Affeldt the final four. Santiago Casilla, still fighting a blister, warmed up in the sixth.

Bochy and Righetti told the relievers that Affeldt, Romo and Javier Lopez will get the ball in the eighth and ninth innings based on matchups. If the Cardinals had lined up differently, Bochy said, Affeldt might have pitched the eighth and Romo the ninth.

Relievers prefer defined roles, but Affeldt said the matchup approach can work in the this 'pen because of its experience. It requires pitchers to think like the manager and know which reserves are sitting in the opposing dugout. Bullpen coach Mark Gardner also reminds them whom they might face and when.

"Tonight could have been chaotic if we didn't understand what was going on, " Affeldt said. "Since we all know what's going on, we can handle it. Everybody is comfortable with the situation."

Above: Buster Posey hit a home run during the sixth inning.
Liz Hafalia

FEATURE

BRANDON CRAWFORD

BY ANN KILLION

THE HOMETOWN KID

The writing on the brick is worn down after 13 seasons of footsteps and a few Champagne showers. You have to know where to look. From the back end of the Willie Mays statue, walk several paces northeast and count 20 bricks over from the King Street sidewalk.

And there it is.

"Mike Lynn Brandon Amy Kaitlin and Jenna Crawford."

How many Giants players have their own brick outside AT&T Park, purchased back when the idea of having a locker on the inside of the building was nothing more than a childhood dream?

One.

Brandon Crawford, the starting shortstop for the San Francisco Giants. Exactly how he dreamed it in his Bay Area backyard.

Crawford is the first local product in years to be drafted by the Giants and developed into a true regular. Danville's Nate Schierholtz got close, but didn't ever lock down a job in right field over the past few seasons. And Monterey's Mike Aldrete was a part-time starter in the outfield in 1987 and '88. But Crawford is a mainstay on this year's division winners, and he grew up with the Giants.

Somewhere in the Crawford family archives is a photo of Aldrete holding 1-year-old Brandon that season. But then again, somewhere in the Crawford family archives are photos of their kids with many former Giants, because the Crawfords were

Above: Brandon Crawford smiles during a Giants team workout at AT&T Park.
Paul Chinn

28 SAN FRANCISCO GIANTS: A RETURN TO THE PINNACLE

Above: Brandon Crawford throws his bat after his game-winning RBI scored Brandon Belt in the ninth inning, giving the Giants a 3-2 win over San Diego in San Francisco. *Lance Iversen*

loyal season-ticket holders, showing up regularly at spring training and fan-photo days.

Mike Crawford, who handles contracts for global defense and security company Northrop Grumman, said his 9-month-old son wasn't bothered by the loud noise in the 1987 playoffs. No one could have predicted that such early exposure would be good training for entering a postseason environment.

Crawford, 25, is an even-keel player and low-key about living out his dream. He acknowledges former Giants shortstop Royce Clayton was his role model, but ballplayers are good at living in the moment, holding the emotion of the big picture at bay.

Family members, however, don't downplay their amazement.

"I got choked up," Lynn Crawford said of the first time she saw her son in a Giants uniform at AT&T. "How many mothers get to see their child fulfill the dream they've had since they were little?"

The Crawfords lived in Menlo Park before moving to Pleasanton in the 1990s. Brandon learned early to bundle up at Candlestick Park. When he was 5 and the Giants announced that they were fleeing Candlestick and moving to Florida, he was devastated; a Chronicle photographer caught his forlorn face in what was considered the final series at the Stick. When Crawford was in middle school, AT&T opened and the family bought a brick in Wil-

Giants Feature: Brandon Crawford   29

Above: A young Brandon Crawford stands next to his father, Mike, who holds a sign with a message for National League President Bill White on Sunday, Sept. 27, 1992, at Candlestick Park. **Tom Levy**

lie Mays Plaza, along with season tickets.

As a fifth-grade teacher, Lynn listened to her son's big dreams and reminded him, "OK, honey, but make sure you do really well in school, too."

Crawford did well enough in both school and baseball at Foothill High to play at UCLA. There, at a freshman athletes' orientation during his first few weeks, he met gymnast Jalynne Dantzscher. Within months, they were dating, and they were married last December. They are expecting their first child, a daughter, in December.

"He says all the time just how fortunate he is to be playing here," Jalynne said.

Crawford made his big-league debut in May 2011, hitting a grand slam in his first game in Milwaukee, but also was sent down for a while to Triple-A ball in Fresno. It was a stressful time, as he tried to nail down the starting job. But the easy-going shortstop wasn't letting the pressure of his testosterone-fueled sport get to him at home.

He and Jalynne rented a one-bedroom, one-bathroom apartment down King Street from the ballpark. Jalynne's twin sister, Janelle, had just started a teaching job in the East Bay and needed a place to live. Brandon and Jalynne had a pullout couch, so why not? When the twins' older sister, Jamie, landed a job coaching gymnastics in the Bay Area, she joined them too, sharing the sofa bed.

Brandon learned not to linger in the bathroom.

"I managed; I grew up with three younger sisters," Crawford said. "So it wasn't that different."

In the offseason, the newlyweds moved to a

house in Walnut Creek – four bedrooms and two bathrooms – and the sisters came along, though both moved back to Southern California over the summer. Crawford is too young to remember "Three's Company," but knows the general premise. He said the reality of "Four's Company," sharing a home with three sisters, was a lot less wacky than a sitcom.

"It almost seemed natural to me," he said.

The sisters kept Jalynne company when Brandon was traveling, watched the couple's dogs when Brandon and Jalynne were both on the road, and provided benefits that some young ballplayers would love to have, like a clean house, washed and folded laundry and home cooking.

"Baked macaroni and cheese was a big favorite," said Jamie, who did much of the meal planning.

All three sisters were competitive gymnasts at UCLA. Jamie was on the 2000 Sydney Olympic team that won a bronze in 2010 when the third-place Chinese team was ruled to have used underage athletes. Though they didn't handspring or backflip around the house, they did joke with nimble Crawford that he should throw some gymnastics moves into his shortstop repertoire.

"We tease him about throwing in a trick, like a 'Popa,'" Jalynne said, referring to a 360-degree straddle jump named after Romanian gymnast Celestina Popa. "When he's turning a double play and jumping over a guy sliding into second, he could include it."

Crawford's acrobatic turns at shortstop have become his signature, so it was strange to see him struggle with errors early in the season. In the novel "The Art of Fielding," by Chad Harbach, a young shortstop suddenly can't make the throw to first. For a time, early in the season, Crawford seemed to be channeling protagonist Henry Skrimshander, committing 12 errors in his first 60 games.

"I hadn't ever gone through that before, making errors in bunches," Crawford said. "I had some tough plays."

Then the errors all but stopped. He made six in the final 102 games. Crawford had, in effect, two seasons in the field.

"He never hung his head," infield coach Ron

Above: Giants Brandon Belt runs home scoring the winning run off a Brandon Crawford game-winning RBI in the ninth inning. *Lance Iversen*

Wotus said. "I never saw his confidence shaken. He took extra groundballs every day. And he never made excuses."

When he came home from work, Jalynne and her sisters, who learned the need for positive reinforcement in gymnastics, kept their feedback encouraging.

"He never brought it home with him," Jalynne said, adding, "He's a homebody. He likes hanging out, watching movies, playing X-box, playing with the dogs. He cherishes being at home."

And playing at home. When the Giants clinched the National League West on Sept. 22, Crawford's parents, sisters and Jalynne were all in the stands. In the celebration afterward, they came into the clubhouse and saw his locker.

Above it, the nameplate reads Brandon Crawford. Just like the brick outside.

FLASHBACK

PERFECTLY TIMED PENCE HOMER KEYS COMEBACK

■ BY HENRY SCHULMAN

To see Hunter Pence for almost two weeks is to understand that his transmission has no first, second or third gears. He is freeway speed all the way, so it was surprising that he took so long to take a curtain call that Giants fans had been desperate to give him.

Not only that, Melky Cabrera had to push him out of the dugout.

"Those kinds of things happen not too often," Pence said. "Hopefully there's a lot more of that to come."

Stepping to the plate 7-for-51 since being traded, Pence picked a sublime time for his first home run as a Giant on Sunday. His three-run blast off Rafael Betancourt with two outs in the eighth inning broke a just-forged 6-6 tie and gave the Giants a 9-6 comeback victory against the Rockies.

"The dugout was going crazy," shortstop Brandon Crawford said, and it was understandable because the Giants are not a great comeback team. They won for the forth time in 50 tries when trailing after seven innings.

A five-run eighth spared the Giants a depressing series loss against a league doormat ahead of a visit by the majors' best team, the Washington Nationals.

They pop into AT&T Park on Monday night with a 71-44 record fattened by an eight-game win streak that ended Sunday. Three of the their wins came in Washington before the All-Star break in one of the Giants' worst series of the season.

Pence saw Washington a lot, coming from the

National League East. Asked why they are so good, he said with no hint of sarcasm, "Pitching and hitting ... they're good at those."

On Sunday, Barry Zito blew a 3-0 lead produced in the first inning. Zito and George Kontos combined to put the Rockies ahead 5-4 in the sixth, and then Colorado took a 6-4 lead with a gift run off Clay Hensley in the seventh.

But the Giants willed themselves to a feel-good win.

"We needed something like that," Zito said. "We've had a lot of wins by sizable margins and lost some tough ones in-between there. Having come-from-behind wins is important going down the stretch."

Hector Sanchez had a huge hit in the eighth, a pinch double. Angel Pagan walked to load the bases. With one out, Cabrera, who already had two RBIs in the first inning, singled home one run to set up a classic confrontation between Buster Posey and Betancourt, who was summoned to face him.

Posey, who saw 35 pitches in the game, got ahead 3-1, then hit five consecutive fouls before lifting the 10th pitch of the at-bat for a sacrifice fly that tied the game and impressed Pence more than his own home run.

"All the pressure is on Buster because we're down at that point," Pence said. "To wear down the pitcher like that and still get the job done, it's obviously deflating for that pitcher because he just did about 10 wind sprints and we tied the game anyway. That sets the table. There's no pressure on me."

Pressure or not, Pence delivered a blast into the left-field bleachers that roused a crowd of 41,492 into a frenzy. It was Pence's second big moment. In the fifth, he made his best catch as a Giant, racing into the right-center gap to rob Jordan Pacheco and help Zito avoid a big inning.

"This was a big win for us," manager Bruce Bochy said. "You're going to have games like that when you're off, but we found a way to win it. The last thing we wanted to do was lose a series here, especially after the last homestand."

San Francisco Giants' Hunter Pence, right, is congratulated by third base coach Tim Flannery (1) after hitting a three-run home run off Colorado Rockies' Rafael Betancourt in the eighth inning in San Francisco.
AP Photo/Ben Margot

FLASHBACK

NO GOOD IN THIS GOODBYE

■ BY HENRY SCHULMAN

How quickly the winds of change can shift. The Giants figured to face an excruciating decision on Melky Cabrera in November: Should they break with recent precedent regarding position players and commit tens of millions of dollars to a player who figured to have many suitors on the free-agent market?

Now, the question will be different, though equally vexing, and money will not be the guiding factor.

In fact, Cabrera should be available for 10 cents on the dollar for any team that still wants him, and San Francisco might be the best place for him to sign because he built some goodwill among the fans, damaged though that might be now.

Also, Cabrera has proven himself a good enough hitter to warrant the belief that he still can help an offense if he is clean, even if it's not 200 hits worth.

The Giants now face a philosophical question of whether to say "Enough!" and wish Cabrera luck on his next team.

San Francisco is viewed as a steroid epicenter, somewhat unfairly because the use of performance-enhancing drugs was rampant everywhere.

But the BALCO lab was on the Peninsula. Barry Bonds was here, and Giants fans embraced him even as evidence mounted that he was juicing because, dammit, everybody is doing it; he's being singled out only because everybody hates him.

The Mitchell Report was stuffed with Giants

Above: Melky Cabrera tied a Giants record for most hits in a month during their game against the Diamondbacks. *Sarah Rice*

Opposite Page: Cabrera turns to the Giants dugout and voices his displeasure after striking out in the 8th inning. *Lance Iversen*

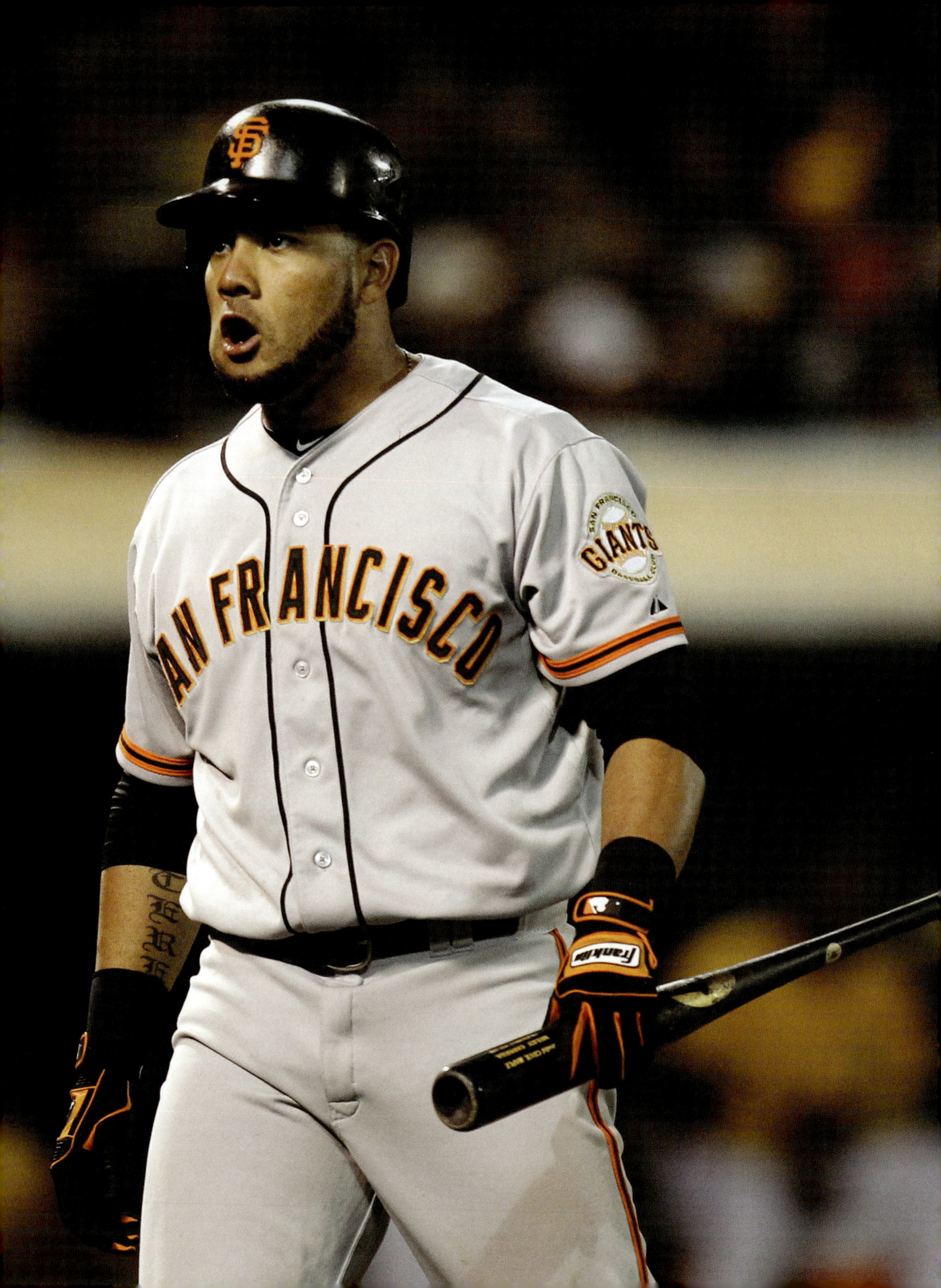
AN FRANCISCO
GIANTS

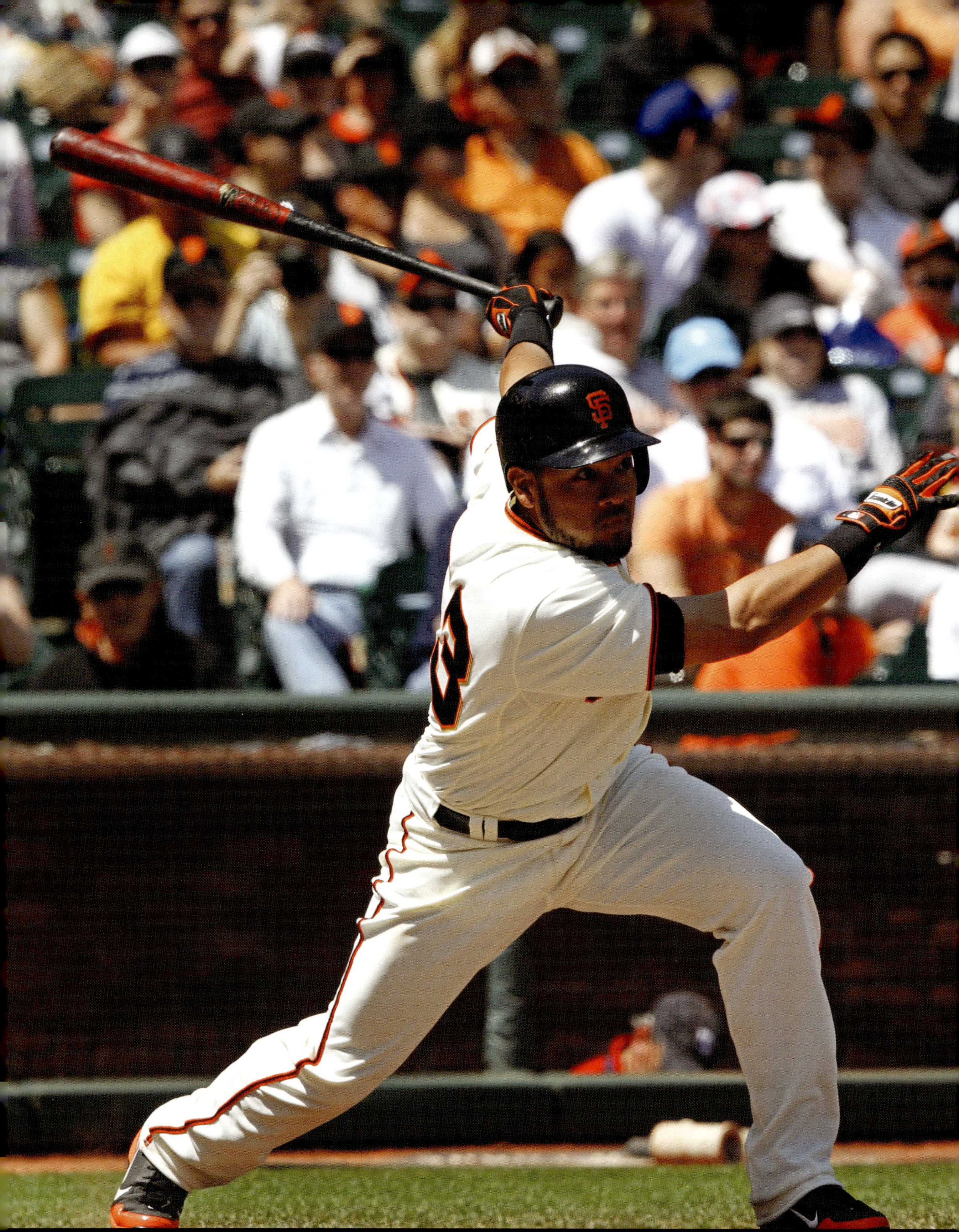

names. It chided the team's management for allegedly looking the other way, which team officials have said was unfair.

The connection did not end with Bonds and the Mitchell Report. Jose Guillen was the Giants' starting right fielder as late as Game 162 of the 2010 championship season until he had to go away because he was being investigated for a shipment of human growth hormone that he allegedly arranged to be shipped to San Francisco.

The Giants signed reliever Guillermo Mota even after he served a 50-game suspension for violating the drug policy in 2007. They believed a player who served his punishment deserved a chance to work, and he had a durable arm.

Mota gave the Giants two good seasons, then got caught again early this season, saying he inadvertently ingested a banned substance by drinking children's cough medicine. He is serving a 100-game suspension that ends this month, and he already is preparing his arm to return.

None of this implies that the Giants openly tolerate drug use or fail to do the proper due diligence in acquiring players, who violate the rules in their own way on their own time. There are no more smoking syringes left in lockers.

Teams cannot install cameras in the players' condos. If these guys want to go the dope route and risk being caught by the Joint Drug Program, the Giants – or any other organization – would be hard-pressed to stop them.

As manager Bruce Bochy correctly said Wednesday, "This is something you can't control. It's been all over baseball."

He also said, "I think the best thing we can do in Major League Baseball is educate these guys and make sure they're informed about situations like this."

But aren't major-leaguers already educated up the wazoo? Shouldn't the suspensions already handed down be listed in the course catalog as Don't Even Think About It 101?

The players know what they're doing and they understand the risks, which evidently still do not outweigh the potential financial rewards in some of their minds.

Back to the original question.

Should the Giants take a stand and say goodbye to Cabrera? Perhaps not even let him participate in any postseason games (if there are any for San Francisco) when he is eligible to return?

If the team wants to "do something about this" and take a big step toward distancing San Francisco from the PED story after nearly 10 years, it has one clear option: to shutter its checkbook when Cabrera or any other suspended player comes calling for a contract.

Should the Giants do it, knowing that a division rival might overlook the suspension and snag him?

That is not a question for the moment. Now, the Giants are focused on surviving the final 44 games of their season and trying to win a division, a pursuit they still owe one another and the fans.

But make no mistake: It's a question the leaders of this franchise would be well served in debating over the months to come.

Below: Cathy Chavez-Miller, left, and Maryanne Paul of Watsonville, wear Milk man hats reading "spoiled Melky" referring to Melky Cabrera's suspension for testing positive for testosterone use. MLB announced the suspension of Melky Cabrera earlier in the day, leaving the Giants without one of their best offensive players and the Giants lost to the Nationals 6-4. Carlos Alvia Gonzalez

FEATURE

BUSTER POSEY

BY ANN KILLION

IT'S ALL ON THE FIELD

Buster Posey is a throwback. Not just in his square-jawed leadership, his 1950s haircut and his stoic toughness. But in his polite unwillingness to tear back the curtain on his personality, to reveal his fears and hopes and dreams, to submit to psychoanalysis by sports media.

In interviews he answers questions, reveals little and seems quite eager to have that part of his job completed and return to analyzing film of opposing hitters and resuming the squat.

For sportswriters, Posey makes our job tough. The Giants serve up platefuls of drama in the form of thongs and beards, steroid scandals and anxiety disorders, rousing speeches and wobbly confidence. Posey has not participated in any of those storylines. Even his most gut-wrenching and intensely human narrative – a grisly injury, painful rehabilitation and triumphant comeback – has been strictly business, a matter-of-fact accomplishment. If anyone wants to shade it in deep hues of drama and emotion, Posey is not providing the Crayolas. We're on our own.

But Posey has become the most compelling figure on the team the old-fashioned way.

By the strength of what he does on the field.

This week he entered the national conversation about the best players in the game. It's one thing to compile awards and statistics: Rookie of the Year, winner of the 2012 batting title, presumptive MVP, potential Comeback Player of the Year.

Above: Catcher Buster Posey puts on his gear before the San Francisco Giants Cactus League spring training game. It was Posey's first game since his season-ending ankle injury last May. *Paul Chinn*

Opposite Page: Buster Posey catches Atlanta Braves Reed Johnson ball behind the plate in the sixth inning of their MLB baseball game. Giants won 5-3. *Lance Iversen*

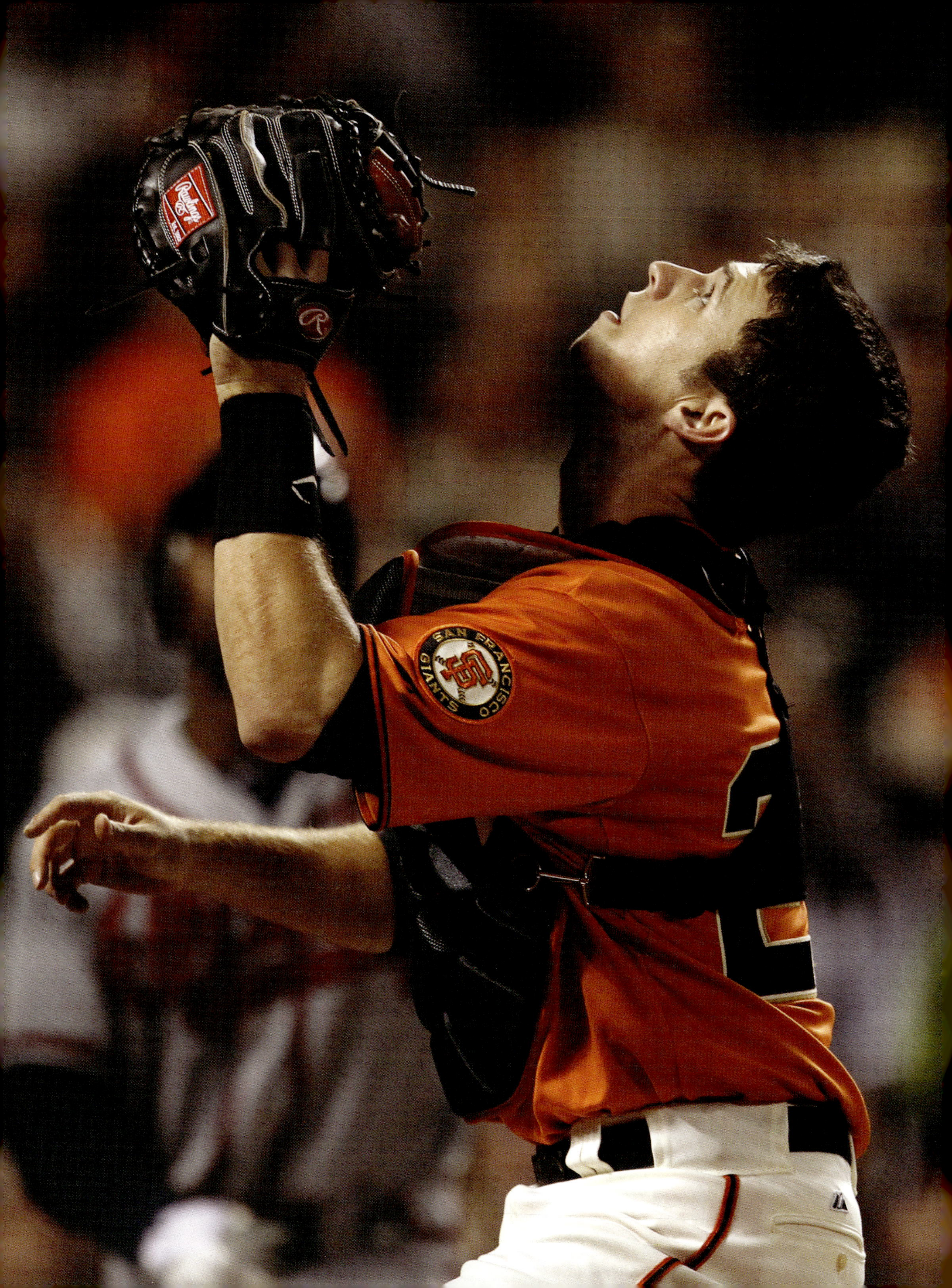
SAN FRANCISCO GIANTS

Above: Giants' Buster Posey escapes a spray of champagne as the team celebrates in the clubhouse, as the San Francisco Giants beat the Cincinnati Reds 6-4 in Game 5 to win the National League Division Series in Cincinnati. *Michael Macor*

It's another to deliver for your team in the heat of the playoffs in a scene out of "The Natural." A soaring 434-foot grand slam that caromed off the scoreboard at Cincinnati's Great American Ball Park. All that was missing was exploding electrical fireworks into the night sky - hey, it was a day game - as Captain America rounded the bases.

While the blast didn't guarantee Posey's spot in Cooperstown, it captured the attention of the baseball world. Because that's what superstars do: They come up big in the postseason.

Around here, where Posey T-shirts and jerseys bloom on almost every back, we didn't need that monster grand slam to understand Posey's impact. As a rookie, he stepped into a leadership role in late May of 2010, taking charge of a dominant pitching staff, hitting cleanup and leading his team to a World Series victory.

Two years later, his teammates are still astonished by what he did at age 23.

40   SAN FRANCISCO GIANTS: A RETURN TO THE PINNACLE

"I've never seen any young man come in with the responsibility that he had, " Giants pitcher Jeremy Affeldt said.

Posey's follow-up to the World Series was one of omission. When he was injured in a home plate collision, almost one year after he joined the team as a regular, and was lost for the season, the Giants foundered. Without Posey, they were no longer a postseason team.

This year, he's back. Behind the plate. Leading the team with his bat. Calmly solving all of the Giants' most burning concerns from seven months ago. He was an All-Star (it no longer looks like ballot-stuffing), led the team down the stretch, filled the void – and the batting title – left by Melky Cabrera, and overcame all doubters of his MVP credentials by the end of the regular season.

The only head-scratcher on his otherwise pristine resume is the reluctance of two of the team's five starting pitchers to throw to him. Whatever the unspoken reasons are behind the catching preference of Barry Zito and Tim Lincecum, Manager Bruce Bochy has done a good job of refusing to let them become a public or clubhouse issue. And the guess here is that those reasons have more to do with the quirks of the pitchers than a deficiency in Posey's game.

Posey said Thursday that Hunter Pence's rousing speeches were the key to the National League Division Series – Pence shook the dust and rust off his flat teammates, verbally slapping them across the face like Cher in "Moonstruck" and shouting "Snap out of it!" That's a great story line, and it's nice to know that Posey appreciates the kind of speech he is unlikely to ever give. But Posey's quiet influence also changed the momentum of the series.

In the critical Game 3, in the bottom of the first, Posey grabbed a wild pitch and threw out Brandon Phillips at third. In a game in which every run was critical, one that wouldn't be decided until a passed ball and error in the 10th, that might have been the difference.

Posey did it again in Game 5, gunning down Jay Bruce at third in the sixth to complete a strikeout-throwout double play to get the Giants out of the inning, a play that Reds manager Dusty Baker said

Above: Buster Posey in the batter's box for his first at-bat at AT&T Park since his season ending injury in May 2011.
Carlos Avila Gonzales

"changed the whole ballgame." Bochy agreed, saying the play "turned things around."

Bochy, an old catcher, leans on his young player.

"He's a leader on this club, " Bochy said. "He leads by example. He's a calming influence."

That's all baseball stuff. The quick turn on a 2-2 fastball. The perfect throw to third to get the runner. The calm work on the field.

That's Buster Posey. That's all you need to know.

FLASHBACK

PAGAN STEPS UP IN TIME OF NEED

■ BY BRUCE JENKINS

Angel Pagan wears the look of a desperate man, a survivor. In fact he's a competent, self-assured professional, but he doesn't so much take the field as he prowls it, catlike, looking just as dangerous as he can. And he's having one hell of an effect on the National League West right now.

During the Giants' three-game sweep in Los Angeles, the Dodgers had the stifling misfortune of trailing in all 27 innings – thanks to Pagan's scoring in each of the first innings. With Buster Posey out of the lineup Thursday night and Melky Cabrera a distant afterthought, the Giants needed more of Pagan's restless energy as they opened a four-game home series against Atlanta.

Not a problem. When people talk about Brian Sabean's best trades over the past three years, they'd better start including Andres Torres to the Mets for Pagan, a disappointment in New York and a budding lifesaver in San Francisco.

The beauty of Pagan is that there's nothing he can't do. He'll hit for power, shoot line drives into the gaps, steal bases, adroitly play the field. In a season of great catches – think Gregor Blanco in Matt Cain's perfect game and Justin Christian just two nights ago in L.A. – Pagan weighed in with a sensational grab against the Padres a month ago, snaring Carlos Quentin's drive to deep left-center and turning it into a double play.

At the moment, he's a run-scoring machine, carrying the team with a catalyst's touch. He led off Thursday night's game with a single, and although the Giants couldn't cash in, he was just getting warmed up. He worked Tommy Hanson for a one-out walk in the third, stole second and scored the game's first run on Pablo Sandoval's single.

"It means a lot to get that from the leadoff position," said first baseman Brandon Belt. "A lot of

Above: Angel Pagan hits an RBI triple driving in Gregor Blanco. *Thearon W. Henderson/Getty Images*

Opposite Page: Angel Pagan slides into home plate to score on a single hit by Pablo Sandoval. *AP Photo/Jae C. Hong*

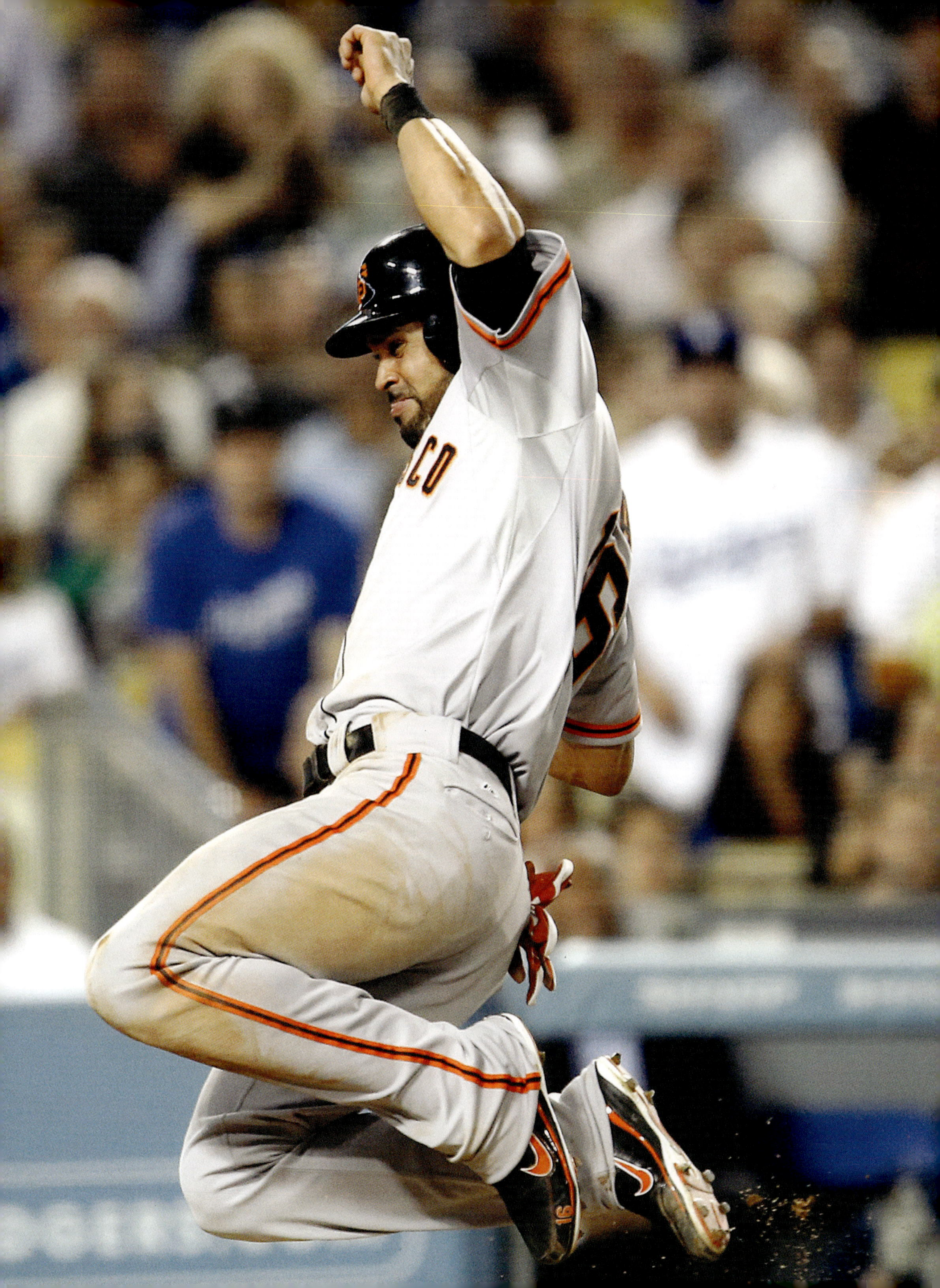

Above: Angel Pagan is safe at second as second baseman Mark Ellis shows his glove. *AP Photo/Jason Redmond*

Opposite Page: Angel Pagan scores sliding past catcher Brian McCann. *Photo by Thearon W. Henderson/Getty Images*

guys have stepped up (since Cabrera's departure) – (Joaquin) Arias, (Marco) Scutaro, and definitely Pagan. It's always our goal to get on the board early, because if we score first, we know we have a good chance to win the game. He's really been setting the tone."

Pagan walked again to lead off the fifth, when the Giants' four-run rally put the game away. The next hitter was Scutaro, whose compact stroke has been another big reason behind the club's recent surge. The beauty of Scutaro is that he'll turn on an inside pitch and hit a dead-pull rocket; teams have to respect that. Lately, though, he's perfected an off-field approach that tormented the Dodgers and, Thursday night, produced a perfect hit-and-run single to right.

As a team that might not hit another homer at home all season (just kidding, though you really have to wonder), the Giants rely on guile and creativity. It's a maddening strategy when it fails, but sometimes the execution produces a slice of pure magic. Such was the case on Hunter Pence's visit to no-man's land.

There were runners at first and third with one out when Pence, who had looked foolish waving at a Hanson curveball in his third-inning strikeout, cast aside his role (he was batting cleanup) and pushed

44   SAN FRANCISCO GIANTS: A RETURN TO THE PINNACLE

a bunt to the right side. This play is an automatic single if the ball gets past the pitcher: too much ground for the second baseman to cover and too risky for the first baseman, who needs to stay on the bag. Pence's bunt went exactly to that spot, and like everyone else who pulled it off, he had to be thinking to himself, "If I could do that every time, I'd bat a thousand."

This was strictly Pence's idea, by the way. "I was as surprised as anybody, " said manager Bruce Bochy. "He told me later he'd done it before. When you're not locked in at the plate, you'll do anything you can. He put that thing down perfectly."

It's remarkable to consider what the Giants have accomplished since last Wednesday. They became the game's biggest story, thanks to the Cabrera suspension, and an ugly gray cloud smothered the organization. It didn't take long for the players to realize they'd be on their own, left to reach the postseason without their best hitter, but that's a mission any club would undertake. The trick was to prove their worth on the field, and they've won six out of their last seven games in a flurry of timely hits and great pitching.

To have Barry Zito join the party, throwing shutout ball against a tough Braves lineup over the first eight innings, is enough to make fans believe that anything is possible. There's no telling what the rest of the season might bring, but in less than a week, the Giants have thoroughly dispatched their post-Melky depression. It lasted maybe 24 hours, tops. That's the mark of a team with serious intent.

FLASHBACK

MAKING A SEPTEMBER PITCH

BY HENRY SCHULMAN

The Tim Lincecum who owned the majors' worst ERA by a starter in the first half has vanished. For that, a team whose heralded rotation is not purring like a fine-tuned engine can be thankful.

Lincecum carried a ghastly 6.42 ERA into the All-Star break. He has the best number on the Giants' staff since at 3.33.

These are not just abstract statistics. As the Giants march toward a National League West title, which gained more inevitability with Wednesday night's series-clinching, 8-3 victory over the Rockies, Lincecum is making a strong case that even if he is not the Freak of old he can still be an effective postseason starter.

"He's really elevated his game and gotten on track here, which is huge for us, " manager Bruce Bochy said, "the way he's throwing the ball and winning games for us. Now we have a couple of guys who have had hiccups, and he's helped pick us up."

With the Dodgers losing again, Lincecum's six-inning, three-run win helped widen the gap in the National League West, which the Giants lead by seven games.

He struck out eight to raise his season total to 177 in 169 2/3 innings. No. 177 was something special.

After scoring five runs in the first inning, the Giants' lead was cut to 6-3 after Charlie Blackmon's RBI double in the sixth. Bochy jogged to the mound with two outs not to yank Lincecum but to tell

Above: Lincecum delivers against the Rockies at Coors Field and earned the win as the Giants defeated the Rockies 8-3 *AP Photo/Jae C. Hong*

Above: Starting pitcher Tim Lincecum of the Giants delivers against the Rockies at Coors Field. Doug Pensinger/Getty Images

him, "It's your game right now. Focus on your pitches."

Lincecum needed only three to whiff Dexter Fowler, a slider, curveball and fastball.

Asked about the trajectory of his turnaround this season, Lincecum said, "It feels good, obviously. From a personal standpoint you want to be getting better as the year goes on, getting better as the last month is coming up.

"Right now I'm not pitching great, but I'm getting out of jams, which is a lot different than what I was used to in the first half."

Lincecum's biggest task now is trying to eliminate an abundance of walks that have him "messing with fire, " as he put it.

On Wednesday he extended, then ended a streak of 10 consecutive innings with at least one walk, the longest by a Giant in 36 years. He walked 11 Cubs, Dodgers and Rockies over the 10 innings, but only two contributed to runs.

Though that gives Lincecum the confidence of a scrambler, he also has to know those walks would kill him against the high-powered Washington and Cincinnati offenses, the Giants' likeliest first-round playoff foes.

Bochy is taking no chances getting there. He used seven relievers to get the final nine outs and brought in Javier Lopez and Sergio Romo in the ninth with a five-run lead.

The stadium DJ played Dolly Parton's "Here You Come Again" when he made pitching change No. 5.

"I'm showing respect for their team in this ballpark, " Bochy said. "I've been here for a few comebacks. You don't (let them) get a rally started. When you get momentum going, it's hard to stop."

Just ask Rockies starter Jeff Francis, who allowed a Gregor Blanco triple on the game's second pitch and watched the Giants tag him for five runs, the big hit a two-run Brandon Crawford double.

The Giants, who finished 7-2 at Coors Field, are going to miss this place. They've scored 76 of their 631 runs here.

FLASHBACK

GIANT STEP

BY AL SARACEVIC

In the end, it was more of a cinch than a clinch. The 2012 edition of the San Francisco Giants won the Western Division title against the San Diego Padres, just as their 2010 championship predecessors did. But the comparisons stop there.

In 2010, the team was known for torturing its fans. The clincher came in the last game of the season. The score was 3-0, and it was tighter than that.

This year's squad provided constituents with the spa treatment. The Giants rolled to an 8-4 win that was not that close. They clinched the title with 10 games to spare. Their biggest worry is how to stay sharp.

As the players partied and celebrated on the field after the win, Giants President and CEO Larry Baer was hugging every Giant he could find. "The players are all saying we need three more hugs," said Baer, between hugs. They'll need to win three postseason series to get in all that hugging, of course.

At least they'll be plenty rested. This season's division title hasn't been in doubt for about two weeks, really. It was only a matter of when. Apparently, manager Bruce Bochy had no interest in intrigue. He wanted to give the players some rest before the postseason, which should give all the sports wonks plenty to wag about: Did they peak too early? Are they going in hungry? How do you line up your rotation? And all the other blather.

In reality, this year's Giants are a better vintage of baseball team than 2010's. This team deserved to win comfortably.

"It feels way different," said Pablo Sandoval, reflecting on 2010 as Emmanuel Burriss poured Champagne down the back of his shirt. "We started low this year. But it's how you finish."

Above: Sergio Romo celebrates the final San Diego Padres out as the Giants clinch the NL west with an 8-4 win. *Lance Iversen*

This year's Giants finished strong. Stronger than the 2010 version, in reality.

For one, they hit better. The 2012 Giants have scored 679 runs in 152 games. The 2010 champs scored 697 in 10 more games. Last year's putrid offense – without Buster Posey – scored a mere 570. Beyond those basic numbers, this lineup is surging of late. Marco Scutaro is channeling Rogers Horn-

48   SAN FRANCISCO GIANTS: A RETURN TO THE PINNACLE

Right: Giants' Pablo Sandoval falls over the railing after catching San Diego Padres' Yonder Alonso's foul ball in the fourth inning.
Lance Iversen

sby at second base. Posey brings Johnny Bench to mind. And Pablo Sandoval? Well, he's an original. (Maybe if Tony Gwynn had played third?)

For two, their pitching has seasoned. Madison Bumgarner's solid start on clinch night topped off a season in which he emerged. Matt Cain has been a rock. At times, a perfect rock. Tim Lincecum has bounced back from a terrible start. And Barry Zito and Ryan Vogelsong are in a horse race for the No. 4 postseason rotation spot, both making compelling stretch runs.

Third, they're younger. This team is Posey and Sandoval and Cain and Bumgarner and Brandon Belt and Brandon Crawford. There's not a codger in the bunch.

"This year's a completely different feeling," said Aubrey Huff, the heart of the 2010 squad and one of this year's few oldsters. "We didn't have this kind of lead. It's a lot more relaxing this way."

You could feel the relaxation throughout Saturday's game.

The mood was tense yet subdued. It was as if expectation had replaced hope. Satisfaction subbing for anxiety.

When Posey came up with the bases loaded and no outs in the first inning, it almost seemed too easy. He delivered only a sacrifice fly, but the place settled into a mellow reverie until the top of the fourth when Sandoval hurled himself over a railing to catch a foul ball ... while blowing a bubble. The place erupted and kept a healthy buzz for the rest of the night.

But it wasn't 2010. When Journey's "Lights" played over the sound system in the eighth inning, the crowd sang along in self-satisfaction. But a little bit of that old magic seemed missing.

And one could say that's the key question. They have the talent. But can this year's Giants procure the same pixie dust that Huff and Pat Burrell and Cody Ross and Edgar Renteria found? Those were some hungry old players, some fighting for their last chance at the big prize.

This year's crew overcame injury (Brian Wilson), scandal (Melky Cabrera) and greed (Los Angeles Dodgers).

Can they achieve destiny?

FLASHBACK 49

FEATURE

SERGIO ROMO

■ BY ANN KILLION

2-PITCH DUEL IN NLDS – A LOOK INTO ROMO'S MAKEUP

Pitch 1.
Sergio Romo held the Giants in his right hand, their fate hanging between his release point and Buster Posey's mitt. Two men on, one out, the Giants' lead shrunk to two runs and Cincinnati's powerful Jay Bruce at the plate. Get the out and keep playing. Give up a home run and go home. The moment, in Game 5 of the NLDS, was the biggest of Romo's career.

"By far the most difficult thing I've ever done, " he said Monday." It's the obligation to be something more than maybe you are."

Bruce fouled off the first pitch. Romo was ahead 0-1. It was going to be a journey.

Pitch 2. Foul. 0-2.

Why was Romo, 29, even facing Bruce, a left-handed power hitter? Not long ago, Romo was considered a right-handed specialist, not trustworthy enough to face a big left-handed hitter. And not much longer before that, some wondered if he was trustworthy enough even to make it to the big leagues.

"There was a lot of maturing," said Bobby Evans, the Giants' vice president of baseball operations. "Following rules and regulations was not the easiest thing for him."

Pitch 3. Outside. 1-2.

In the lettuce fields of Salinas, Sergio's father, Frank, became a Giants fan. Born in Mexico and

Above: Pitcher Sergio Romo jokes with his teammates befor a game with the Miami Marlins. *Lance Iveren*

Opposite page: Closer Sergio Romo makes the final out to end the game, as the San Francisco Giants beat the St. Louis Cardinals 7-1. *Michael Macor*

50 SAN FRANCISCO GIANTS: A RETURN TO THE PINNACLE

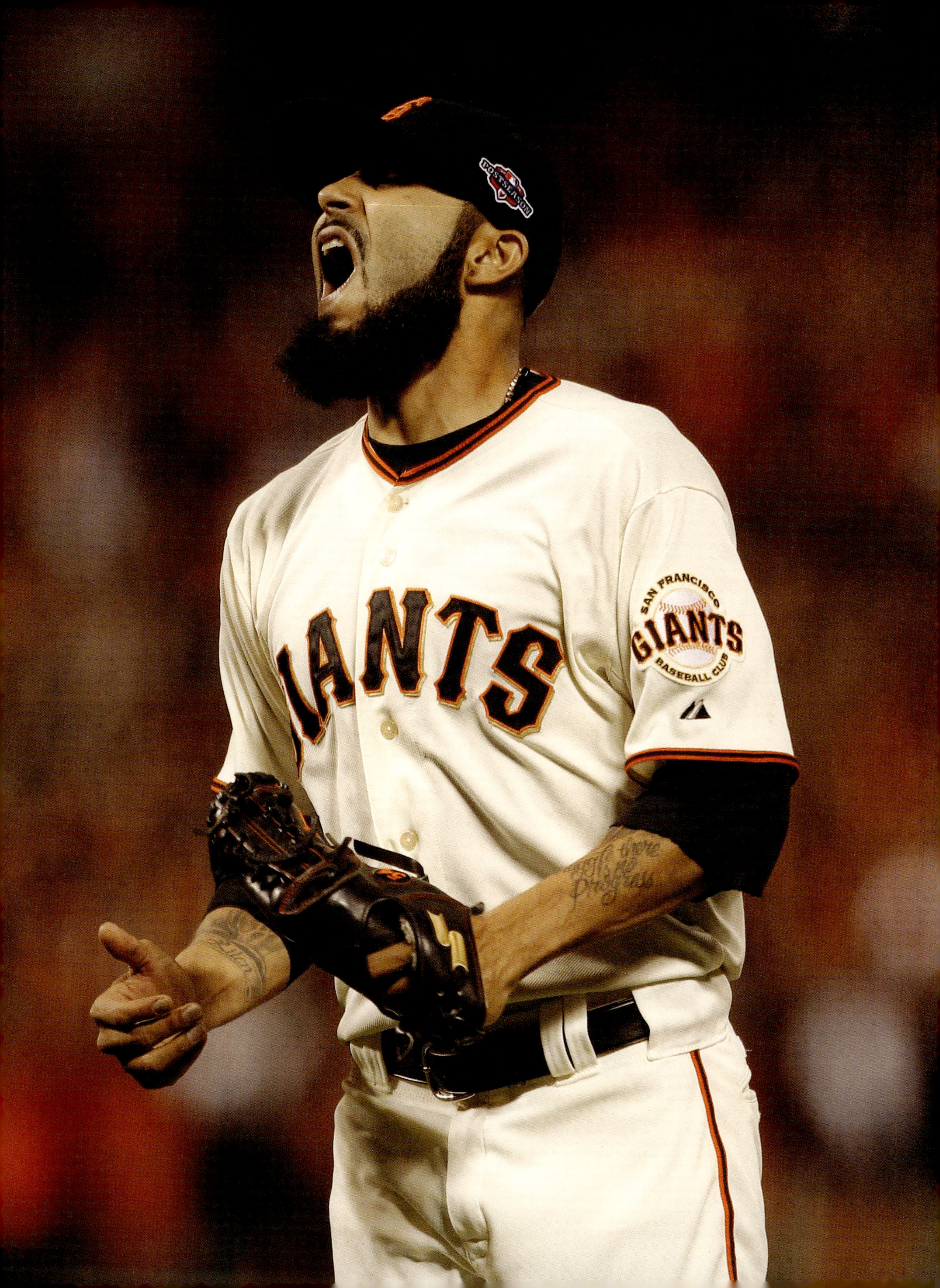
SAN FRANCISCO
GIANTS
BASEBALL CLUB

Above: Sergio Romo massages his beard during the eighth inning of a Milwaukee Brewers game in San Francisco Calif.
Lance Iversen

raised in the Imperial Valley, Frank's family headed north every summer, following the crops. In the summer of 1969, Frank went to Candlestick Park to see Willie Mays, the greatest player who ever lived. Frank Romo became a Giants fan for life.

He gave Sergio his first glove and taught him to play catch when the boy was 2. Frank played semi-pro ball across the border in Mexicali, bringing along little Sergio.

"There's more to this game than just the physical part," Frank said. "He loves the game. I always tell him, '*Hijo*, you have so much heart.'"

Pitch 4. Foul. 1-2.

Brawley – in the southeast corner of California, 23 miles from the Mexican border – isn't a town that invites opportunity. Or baseball scouts. It's the type of town where ambition can be squashed.

"They look at my face, at my size, at the color of the skin, at where I came from, what I grew up as," Romo said. "It's all outside stuff, stuff that doesn't really matter."

Romo played baseball and sought thrills. He raced BMX bikes and once sustained a severe concussion and broken collarbone and was airlifted to a trauma center. He missed the rest of his baseball season.

That wasn't his only collision: He mouthed off to opponents, ignored rules, was kicked out of practice.

"Me and authority don't get along," Romo said. "I've never done things by the book."

Pitch 5. Foul. 1-2.

The matchup looked distorted, like a movie special effect when Hagrid looms over Harry Potter. Romo, at 5-foot-10, on the mound. Bruce, at 6-3, swelling over the plate like a cartoon.

The few scouts who saw Sergio in high school dismissed him as being too small. He asked Frank, "Why didn't you make me 6 feet?" He had no offers from a four-year school.

Pitch 6. Foul. 1-2.

Frank urged his son to follow his path and join the Navy.

"It toughened me up, helped me grow as a man," Frank said. "I figured that could happen to him."

A signature away from enlisting, Romo balked. He persuaded Frank to let him try to play college ball, beginning his enrollment in what Romo calls "Pick-a-year University." Four colleges in four years. First stop, Orange Coast College. Then Arizona Western, North Alabama and Mesa State.

Pitch 7. Foul. 1-2.

Romo's toughest year was his junior year in Florence, Alabama. He and the coach butted heads. When he was about to break the school record for strikeouts, the coach pulled him from a game, telling him he didn't deserve the honor.

"I was reminded every day that I was different," he said. "I was uncoachable to him."

Romo lost his scholarship.

Pitch 8. Foul. 1-2.

The day Romo left Alabama, some old teammates put in a word for him at Mesa State, in Grand Junction, Colo. Romo told coach Chris Hanks the unvarnished truth about Alabama. The coach appreciated his honesty and offered him a scholarship.

"He took a chance on a kid just doing what his dad taught him to do: be honest," Romo said. "That was my biggest turning point."

In Grand Junction, Romo went 14-1 and broke six school records. He didn't even know his stats. He was simply having fun.

Pitch 9. Low and outside. 2-2.

The Giants drafted Romo in the 28th round in 2005. He balked at the rules in the minor leagues, breaking curfew, leaving without permission, getting angry enough to punch a wall and break his hand. The Giants left him in extended spring training.

"That was really hard for him," Evans said. "He wanted to get out of there and get in our program. But he had to wait and wait and wait."

Pitch 10. Foul. 2-2.

In 2007, Romo had a standout season with San Jose, named the Class A Relief Pitcher of the Year. He made his big-league debut in 2008 and established a reputation as a dominant right-handed reliever. By the time the Giants won a World Series, he was a fan favorite.

"He's extremely popular," Evans said. "He's very compassionate. There's nothing fake about him."

Pitch 11. Inside. 3-2.

Before this year, Romo had all of three big-league saves and was in awe of the pressure Brian Wilson faced nightly. But as the season evolved and closer-by-committee became closer-by-Romo, he listened to his locker neighbor.

"He told me to just get the outs," Romo said. "Be confident. He's helped calm my emotions."

In Game 3 of the NLDS, Bruce Bochy leaned on Romo for the final six outs. On Thursday, Bochy didn't waver, saying that if the team went down, it would be with its best reliever on the mound.

Pitch 12.

A slider Bruce lifted into left field. Xavier Nady drifted under it, corralling the ball. Two outs. Romo walked behind the mound and licked his fingers. Back in Brawley, Frank and Sergio's mother, Leticia, were screaming and weeping.

"The precision, the focus, the game plan," Evans said. "He wasn't going to give in. He kept pounding the same spot, again and again.

"To see how he's evolved, the stamina, the strength, the mental capacity, the emotional control. The way he's overcome the odds. It's a beautiful thing."

After the epic duel, the final out came after five pitches. Romo struck out Scott Rolen and howled with joy as his teammates rushed at him.

"The most gratifying moment," Romo said, "was after I got out of the pile. I looked back and saw them jumping around and laughing and smiling. To know that I was part of that smile.

"They relied on me and it actually worked."

FEATURE

BARRY ZITO

■ BY BRUCE JENKINS

GEM BRINGS SERIES HOME

The truth about the Giants is that they have no home. They're the most comfortable travelers baseball has seen in years. They check out of hotels with great reluctance, pining for just one more day with those tiny bars of soap.

The fact that they will be home, for a Game 6 of the National League Championship Series on Sunday, gives this postseason a special place in franchise history. They've already done enough to defy convention, the odds and rampant skepticism. It's only right that this series plays to a conclusion in front of the fans who have packed AT&T Park all season.

If you don't quite recognize the team that hung a stunning 5-0 defeat on the St. Louis Cardinals on Friday night, it's because the Giants have established a postseason pattern too indelible to deny. On top of Barry Zito's epic Game 5 performance and the three-game sweep in Cincinnati, they clinched all of their 2010 playoff series – against Atlanta, Philadelphia and Texas – on the road.

It was a night of raw desperation for the Giants, their deeds downright heroic at times. Zito, with his $7^{2}/_{3}$ innings of six-hit, shutout ball, didn't just pitch "his best game as a Giant," said former owner Peter Magowan, standing proudly in a corner of the winning clubhouse. In terms of postseason elimination games, it was the greatest performance ever by a Giants starter.

The clubhouse reaction to Zito's performance bordered on reverence. "When you think about all

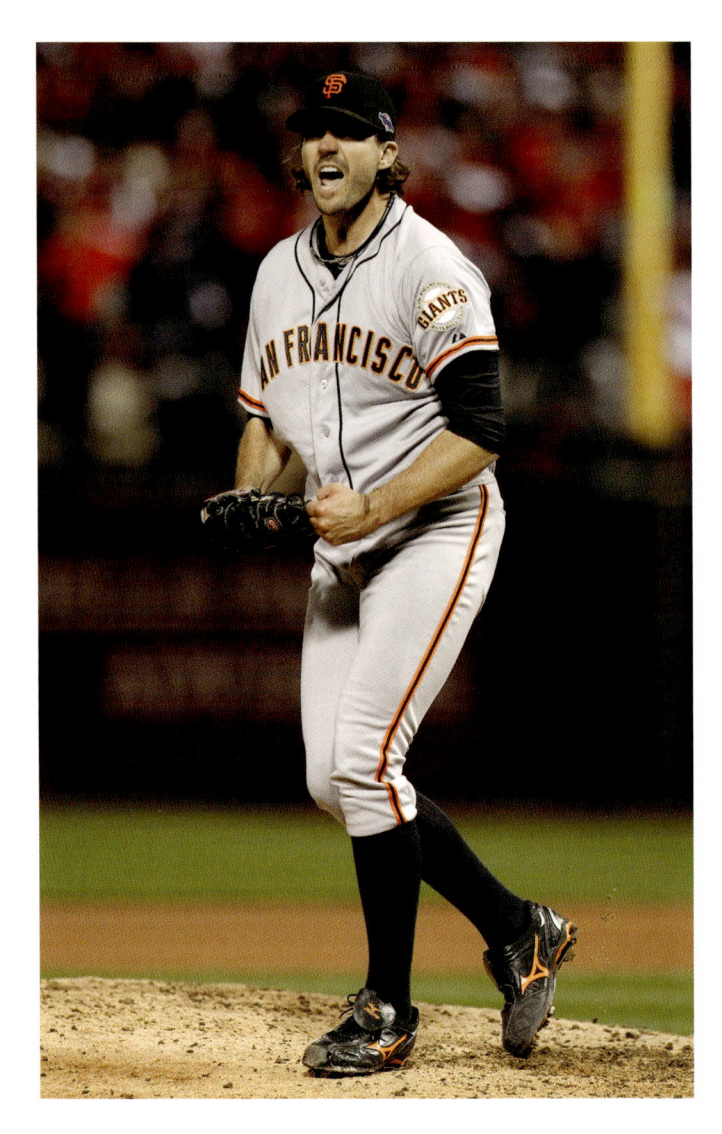

Above: Giants' pitcher Barry Zito lets out a yell as he strikes out the Cardinals' Pete Kozma to end the seventh inning, as the San Francisco beat St. Louis 5-0 in Game 5 of the National League Championship Series. *Michael Macor*

54 SAN FRANCISCO GIANTS: A RETURN TO THE PINNACLE

Above: Giants' starting pitcher, Barry Zito throws as the Giants take on the St. Louis Cardinals in game five of the National League Championship Series. *Michael Macor*

he's gone through," said reliever Jeremy Affeldt, "the tough times, not making the playoff roster two years ago, for him to come in this year and win 15 games, knowing he's under the microscope every time he pitches, and now here's our biggest game of the year, and he does that – I'll be proud to say I was there."

Zito ranks with the truly awful hitters in the game, but he's fairly adroit on bunt attempts. He dropped a beautiful sacrifice bunt in the third inning, then shocked everyone with a drag-bunt single down the third-base line in the fourth, driving in a run and making it clear this was a special evening.

"I've seen him try it a couple of times, but not quite like that," manager Bruce Bochy said. "Couldn't have put it in a better spot. That surprised a lot of people, including us."

Zito's improvisation inspired a remarkable sequence of events. Second baseman Marco Scutaro made a fabulous play in the fifth inning only moments after Hunter Pence's once-in-a-lifetime play on a lazy fly ball down the right-field line.

On the dead run, and about to slide, Pence knew he'd need two hands to cover all the possibilities – and the ball struck his bare hand first, before caroming straight into the glove. "No matter how many baseball games you watch, you always see something new," said a beaming Pence.

That's the thing about elimination games, said Affeldt. "When athletes are backed up against the wall, we're gonna do whatever we gotta do. Zito's bunt – that was a gutsy deal, man. Pence makes that catch, out of nowhere. Sometimes when you're playing a team that's in a hole, like we are, it's hard to beat 'em."

Giants Feature: Barry Zito

NLDS GAME 1

FAILING TO SEIZE AN OPENING

■ BY HENRY SCHULMAN

The 2010 postseason started with something magical when Tim Lincecum struck out 14 in a shutout of Atlanta at AT&T Park. There was magic inside for the 2012 postseason opener as well. You just had to be wearing red to enjoy it. Cincinnati beat the Giants and Matt Cain 5-2 Saturday night after overcoming the kind of blow that can cripple a team when starter Johnny Cueto had to leave eight pitches into the first inning with back spasms.

The Giants got a huge break, not having to face the third-place finisher in the National League ERA race and forcing the Reds to scramble for 26 outs.

Rather than scramble, four Cincinnati pitchers suffocated the Giants for $8^{2/3}$ innings and brought the Reds their first postseason win since 1995.

Longtime Giants nemesis Mat Latos, who had been scheduled to start Game 3 in Cincinnati, took the ball on three days' rest. Pitching in relief for the first time since Class A ball in 2009, he held San Francisco to a Buster Posey solo homer in four innings.

The Reds' three-headed bullpen monster – Sean Marshall, Jonathan Broxton and Aroldis Chapman – finished the job, though the Giants scored on a passed ball before Chapman struck out Posey on a high fastball to end it.

Any real shot of a comeback against Chapman died when Santiago Casilla allowed two runs in the ninth, one on a Posey passed ball.

The Giants now face a hard climb after dropping Game 1, which they did not do in their three 2010 postseason series. They need to win three of the final four games, at least two in Cincinnati.

"It'll be fine," Cain said. "We'll find out what tomorrow brings. Today is done with."

Cain allowed his first earned runs in the postseason after pitching $21^{1/3}$ innings without allowing one in 2010, and he lost to the Reds for the third time this year – half of his six defeats.

Home runs were a story in the two regular-season games, and they were again Saturday. Brandon Phillips hit one with a runner aboard in the third inning, and Jay Bruce lined a solo shot in the fourth.

Above: Marco Scutaro misses a tag on Brandon Phillips late in the game. *Brant Ward*

Above: Giants pitcher Matt Cain gives up a solo home run to the Reds' Ryan Ludwick in the fourth inning. *Michael Macor*

NLDS GAME 1

Above: Giants center fielder Angel Pagan and teammates head to the clubhouse, as the Giants lose to the Cincinnati Reds 5-2 in Game 1 of the National League Divisional Series. *Michael Macor*

The Phillips homer was the game's biggest swing and ate at Cain because he hung a curveball.

"That's something you don't want to have in a big-game situation," Cain said. "Hanging breaking balls, they always hurt a little more in a postseason game."

Cain was lifted for a pinch-hitter and sat stone-faced in the dugout as Aubrey Huff flied out in his place.

That Cain lasted only five innings and 75 pitches boosts the likelihood that he would pitch Game 4 in Cincinnati on short rest if the Giants face elimination.

If the Giants lose the series, Game 1 will be remembered as the night the Giants let a big gift get away at the outset.

Cueto struck out Angel Pagan with an inside fastball to start his game and got ahead of Marco Scutaro 0-1 when he threw another strike and immediately walked off the mound wincing. He took a few steps toward first base and looked into the sky, knowing he was done.

Hunter Pence said the change of pitcher was "a little bit of a curveball" but insisted Giants hitters did not assume they were in for a cakewalk.

"You know it's going to be a grind," he said. "They've got great pitching. They've got a good bullpen."

Gregor Blanco said the quick change of pitchers befuddled the hitters momentarily, but ultimately the Giants were doomed by pitching just as good. With the Giants down 3-1 in the eighth, Jonathan Broxton threw a good 3-2 fastball that froze Blanco for a strikeout that stranded the potential tying runs.

The Giants and their fans were mortuary silent until the middle of the sixth inning, when the stadium DJ played the Korean rap song "Gangnam Style."

The crowd was still howling when Posey stepped in and hit Latos' first pitch into the left-field seats, cutting the Reds' lead to 3-1. Pence momentarily had the crowd thinking back-to-back, but his high drive to center was caught at the track.

BOX SCORE

Reds 5, Giants 2

Cincinnati	AB	R	H	BI	BB	SO	Avg.
B.Phillips 2b	5	1	3	3	0	0	.600
Cozart ss	4	0	1	0	0	2	.250
Votto 1b	3	0	0	0	1	1	.000
Ludwick lf	3	0	0	0	1	2	.000
Heisey pr-lf	0	0	0	0	0	0	—
Bruce rf	4	1	2	1	0	0	.500
Rolen 3b	4	0	0	0	0	1	.000
Hanigan c	4	1	1	0	0	0	.250
Stubbs cf	4	1	1	0	0	1	.250
Cueto p	0	0	0	0	0	0	—
LeCure p	0	0	0	0	0	0	—
H.Bailey ph	1	0	0	0	0	1	.000
Latos p	1	0	0	0	0	1	.000
Cairo ph	1	0	0	0	0	0	.000
Marshall p	0	0	0	0	0	0	—
Broxton p	0	0	0	0	0	0	—
Paul ph	1	1	1	0	0	0	1.000
A.Chapman p	0	0	0	0	0	0	—
Totals	35	5	9	4	2	9	

Giants	AB	R	H	BI	BB	SO	Avg.
Pagan cf	5	0	1	0	0	1	.200
Scutaro 2b	4	0	0	0	1	0	.000
Sandoval 3b	5	0	1	0	0	0	.200
Posey c	5	1	2	1	0	2	.400
Pence rf	4	0	0	0	0	0	.000
Belt 1b	2	0	0	0	2	0	.000
G.Blanco lf	3	0	2	0	1	1	.667
B.Crawford ss	2	0	0	0	1	1	.000
Arias ph	1	1	1	0	0	0	1.000
M.Cain p	1	0	0	0	0	0	.000
A.Huff ph	1	0	0	0	0	0	.000
Kontos p	0	0	0	0	0	0	—
Theriot ph	1	0	0	0	0	0	.000
Mota p	0	0	0	0	0	0	—
Affeldt p	0	0	0	0	0	0	—
S.Casilla p	0	0	0	0	0	0	—
Nady ph	0	0	0	0	1	0	—
Totals	34	2	7	1	6	5	

Cincinnati	002	100	002	—	5 9 1
Giants	000	001	001	—	2 7 0

E—Rolen (1). **LOB**—Cincinnati 6, Giants 11. **2B**—Bruce (1), G.Blanco (1). **HR**—B.Phillips (1), off M.Cain; Bruce (1), off M.Cain; Posey (1), off Latos. **RBIs**—B.Phillips 3 (3), Bruce (1), Posey (1). **Runners moved up**—Votto, Rolen. **GIDP**—Ludwick. **DP**—Cincinnati 1 (Votto); Giants 1 (Scutaro, B.Crawford, Belt).

Cincinnati	IP	H	R	ER	BB	SO	NP	ERA
Cueto	1/3	0	0	0	0	1	8	0.00
LeCure W, 1-0	1 2/3	1	0	0	2	1	25	0.00
Latos	4	4	1	1	1	1	57	2.25
Marshall H, 1	1	0	0	0	0	0	11	0.00
Broxton H, 1	1	1	0	0	1	1	19	0.00
A.Chapman	1	1	1	1	2	1	28	9.00

Giants	IP	H	R	ER	BB	SO	NP	ERA
M.Cain L, 0-1	5	5	3	3	1	4	75	5.40
Kontos	2	0	0	0	0	1	24	0.00
Mota	1/3	0	0	0	1	6	0.00
Affeldt	2/3	0	0	0	1	0	12	0.00
S.Casilla	1	3	2	1	0	3	28	9.00

Inherited runners-scored—Affeldt 1-0. **IBB**—off LeCure (B.Crawford), off Affeldt (Ludwick). **HBP**—by M.Cain (Cozart). **WP**—A.Chapman 2, S.Casilla. **PB**—Posey. **Umpires**—Home, Phil Cuzzi; First, Brian O'Nora; Second, Gerry Davis; Third, Dan Iassogna; Right, Chad Fairchild; Left, Tom Hallion. **Time**—3:27. **Attendance**—43,492 (41,915).

NLDS GAME 2

RED-FACED BY CINCY, S.F. IN DEEP 0-2 HOLE

■ BY HENRY SCHULMAN

The Giants had 2010 World Series hero Edgar Renteria throw the ceremonial first pitch before Game 2 of their Division Series on Sunday night. Renteria's three-run homer to win the clinching game at Texas two years ago taught the faithful not to give up on anybody.

Now, after going down on two hits in a stunning 9-0 loss to the Reds, the Giants must accomplish the metaphorical equivalent of Renteria hitting that home run with a piano strapped to his back.

In fact, they need to make baseball history to keep their season alive.

Though several teams have overcome 0-2 deficits to win best-of-five series, none has won three con-

Above: Joey Votto slides past Buster Posey waiting for the throw on a Scott Rolen single in the fourth inning. *Carlos Avila Gonzalez*

Opposite Page: Giants pitcher Madison Bumgarner, catcher Buster Posey and pitching coach Dave Righetti talk things over in the second inning. *Michael Macor*

NATIONAL LEAGUE DIVISION SERIES GAME 2   61

NLDS GAME 2

Above: Giants manager Bruce Bochy and players head to the clubhouse after their loss. *Michael Macor*

secutive road games, which the Giants must accomplish under this year's 2-3 format.

Adding to the degree of difficulty: The Reds did not get swept at home all season. In fact, they did not lose any three games in a row.

The last Giants sweep in Cincinnati occurred when the Great American Ball Park was just a dream: the first three games of the 1999 season, at Riverfront Stadium.

After absorbing the worst postseason shutout defeat in franchise history, the players were full of "backs against the wall" platitudes for reporters. But what did they discuss with each other before reporters were allowed inside?

"There hasn't really been a whole lot of talking," losing pitcher Madison Bumgarner said.

What could they talk about? Anyone who watched the Reds crush the Giants in what might have been the final two games of the year at AT&T Park would have a hard time imagining a historic charge in Cincinnati.

The Giants scored two runs over the two games, one on Buster Posey's Game 1 homer off Mat Latos and the other on a wild pitch in the ninth inning of Game 1.

In Game 2, Bronson Arroyo (seven innings), J.J. Hoover and Jose Arredondo held the Giants to a Brandon Belt single and two walks until Pablo Sandoval doubled to extend the game with two outs in the ninth.

Change of scenery? Yeah, the Giants need one. They play the first of three potential elimination games in Cincinnati on Tuesday night. They will work out Monday, weather permitting, and manager Bruce Bochy plans to address the team.

"I know they know what's at stake," Bochy said. "You hate to get beat like that, especially at home, but it happened."

It happened before a crowd of 43,505 that became deathly silent when the Reds hit four singles off Bumgarner in the fourth inning to add three runs to a 1-0 lead, which Ryan Ludwick produced with a second-inning home run.

"That's what the other team's job is, to quiet the crowd down a little bit," said Belt, who broke up Arroyo's perfect game with a two-out single in the fifth inning. "That's what they did here. Our plan is to go to their place and do the same thing."

To do that the Giants have to score early and give Game 3 starter Ryan Vogelsong room to breathe. Matt Cain and Bumgarner did not have that luxury and surrendered a combined seven earned runs in 9 1/3 innings.

In contrast, Arroyo skunked the Giants with his array of offspeed pitches thrown at every imaginable angle. Reds pitchers won with brute force in Game 1 then dropped a velvet hammer in Game 2.

They have kept the Giants' table-setters off base. Angel Pagan is 1-for-9. Marco Scutaro, who ended the regular season with a 20-game hitting streak, is 0-for-8. Pablo Sandoval is 2-for-9 with a pair of two-out hits that led to nothing.

"Obviously things haven't gone the way we expected," Scutaro said quietly. "We just have to go to their place and stay aggressive and change the momentum."

The Reds seem to own that momentum lock, stock and barrel.

After Tim Lincecum held them scoreless for two innings, after some confusion in the dugout over whether Bochy wanted him to begin a rare relief appearance in the sixth, the Reds continued to roll the Giants with a five-run eighth against the bullpen that sent Giants fans to the exits.

That would not have happened in the 2010 postseason, which now seems so long ago.

BOX SCORE

Reds 9, Giants 0

Cincinnati	AB	R	H	BI	BB	SO	Avg.
B.Phillips 2b	5	0	2	1	0	0	.500
Cozart ss	4	0	1	0	0	2	.250
W.Valdez ph-ss	1	0	0	0	0	0	.000
Votto 1b	4	2	3	0	0	1	.429
Frazier 1b-3b	1	0	0	0	0	0	.000
Ludwick lf	3	2	2	1	1	0	.333
Heisey pr-lf	1	1	0	0	0	0	.000
Bruce rf	5	1	1	2	0	0	.333
Rolen 3b	3	1	1	1	1	0	.143
Cairo 1b	0	0	0	0	0	0	.000
Hanigan c	4	1	2	3	0	2	.375
Stubbs cf	4	1	1	1	0	0	.250
Arroyo p	4	0	0	0	0	2	.000
Hoover p	0	0	0	0	0	0	—
Arredondo p	0	0	0	0	0	0	—
Totals	**39**	**9**	**13**	**9**	**2**	**7**	

Giants	AB	R	H	BI	BB	SO	Avg.
Pagan cf	4	0	0	0	0	0	.111
Scutaro 2b	4	0	0	0	0	0	.000
Sandoval 3b	4	0	1	0	0	0	.222
Posey c	2	0	0	0	2	0	.286
Pence rf	4	0	0	0	0	0	.000
Belt 1b	3	0	1	0	0	1	.200
G.Blanco lf	2	0	0	0	0	1	.400
Lincecum p	0	0	0	0	0	0	—
Mijares p	0	0	0	0	0	0	—
S.Casilla p	0	0	0	0	0	0	—
Mota p	0	0	0	0	0	0	—
A.Huff ph	1	0	0	0	0	0	.000
Romo p	0	0	0	0	0	0	—
B.Crawford ss	2	0	0	0	1	1	.000
Bumgarner p	1	0	0	0	0	1	.000
Kontos p	0	0	0	0	0	0	—
Nady lf	2	0	0	0	0	1	.000
Totals	**29**	**0**	**2**	**0**	**3**	**5**	

Cincinnati	010	300	050	—	9	13	0
Giants	000	000	000	—	0	2	0

LOB—Cincinnati 5, Giants 5. **2B**—B.Phillips 2 (2), Bruce (2), Sandoval (1). **3B**—Stubbs (1). **HR**—Ludwick (1), off Bumgarner. **RBIs**—B.Phillips (4), Ludwick (1), Bruce 2 (3), Rolen (1), Hanigan 3 (3), Stubbs (1). **GIDP**—Ludwick. **DP**—Giants 1 (B.Crawford, Scutaro, Belt).

Cincinnati	IP	H	R	ER	BB	SO	NP	ERA
Arroyo W, 1-0	7	1	0	0	1	4	91	0.00
Hoover	1	0	0	0	1	1	19	0.00
Arredondo	1	1	0	0	1	0	27	0.00

Giants	IP	H	R	ER	BB	SO	NP	ERA
Bumgarner L, 0-1	4 1/3	7	4	4	1	4	72	8.31
Kontos	2/3	0	0	0	0	0	2	0.00
Lincecum	2	1	0	0	0	2	25	0.00
Mijares	0	2	3	3	1	0	17	-
S.Casilla	1/3	0	0	0	0	0	5	6.75
Mota	2/3	3	2	2	0	1	14	18.00
Romo	1	0	0	0	0	0	14	0.00

Mijares pitched to 3 batters in the 8th. **Inherited runners-scored**—Kontos 2-0, S.Casilla 1-0, Mota 1-1. **WP**—Arredondo. **Umpires**—Home, Brian O'Nora; First, Gerry Davis; Second, Dan Iassogna; Third, Tom Hallion; Right, Phil Cuzzi; Left, Chad Fairchild. **Time**—3:14. **Attendance**—43,505 (41,915).

NLDS GAME 3

STAYING ALIVE

BY HENRY SCHULMAN

The obituary for 2012 was on the galleys, already proofed, ready for printing as soon as someone yelled "Go." It would have said the Giants' season died quietly after not a thing went right in their Division Series against the Reds. It lies on the galley still because a large roster of Giants, starting with Ryan Vogelsong, did just enough to will the Giants to a 2-1, 10-inning victory in Game 3 at Great American Ball Park, ensuring a Game 4 Wednesday.

Buoyed by an emotional pregame speech by Hunter Pence that sent the clubhouse rollicking in cheers, the Giants played with an intensity that seemed missing in San Francisco and won despite having one hit through nine innings.

"I'm not ready to book a flight to Puerto Rico," Angel Pagan said after the win. "I'm ready to win tomorrow and win the series."

That remains possible after the Giants took advantage of two mistakes the Reds seemed incapable of making in the series.

With two outs in the 10th inning, catcher Ryan Hanigan committed a passed ball that allowed Buster Posey and Pence to advance to third and second. The Giants then broke a 1-1 tie when Scott Rolen, who has eight Gold Gloves, bobbled Joaquin Arias' grounder for an error that allowed Posey to score.

Romo then completed a six-up, six-down performance that allowed the Giants to celebrate.

They still need to win two more here to take the best-of-five series. Suddenly the concept does not sound as laughable because the Reds have a pitching problem.

Above: Giants starting pitcher Ryan Vogelsong throws in the first inning. *Michael Macor*

Opposite Page: Giants closing pitcher Sergio Romo lets out a scream as he celebrates the final out in the bottom of the 10th inning to give the Giants the win. *Michael Macor*

NATIONAL LEAGUE DIVISION SERIES GAME 3

NLDS GAME 3

Above: The Giants' Gregor Blanco is hit by a pitch in the third inning in Game 3 of the National League Division Series in Cincinnati. *Michael Macor*

Game 1 starter Johnny Cueto has an oblique injury and cannot pitch. Mat Latos is so sick with flu that he barely could lift his right arm to shake a television commentator's hand. Manager Dusty Baker would not name a Game 4 starter to face Barry Zito. It could be Mike Leake, who was not supposed to start in the series.

No matter who pitches, the Giants need to divine a way to get some hits.

They had two in Game 2 and only one in the first nine innings of Game 3, a Marco Scutaro single off Homer Bailey in the sixth. They scored their first run Tuesday on a hit batter, walk and Pagan's sacrifice fly.

Credit Vogelsong and the Giants' bullpen for keeping this season alive.

Vogelsong held the Reds to one run in five innings. The game could have slipped away in the first when the Reds scored on a Jay Bruce RBI single. However, with two runners on and two outs,

66 SAN FRANCISCO GIANTS: A RETURN TO THE PINNACLE

Vogelsong made the pitch of his life, his 30th of the inning, striking out Rolen on a full-count fastball.

Vogelsong did not buckle after home-plate umpire Gerry Davis refused to give him a 2-2 fastball that seemed to catch the outside corner.

"I told myself, 'It happened. Get ready to make the next pitch,'" Vogelsong said. "I can't really cry over spilled milk. There were guys on base. I knew I had to make another pitch. Buster put down the finger and I just hit his glove."

Vogelsong and four relievers allowed one more hit through the final nine innings, a Rolen infield single.

Once the Reds spent closer Aroldis Chapman in the ninth, the Giants attacked Jonathan Broxton in the 10th. Posey, 0-for-3, singled to right. Pence hit a broken-bat single through the left side after his left calf cramped. He did not run to first base as much as hobble.

The rally seemed doomed when Brandon Belt and Xavier Nady struck out. It wasn't.

Baker let Broxton pitch to Arias rather than walk him and force Bruce Bochy to have Hector Sanchez hit for Romo. That would have meant Tim Lincecum on the mound in the bottom half.

Arias, asked if he was nervous hitting with the Giants' season on the line, said, "Why? This is baseball. I know what to do in this situation."

Reminded he had not faced this situation in a postseason game, Arias said he had a lot of pressure at-bats in Dominican winter ball. He also ended the eighth with a super running catch in the outfield to rob Bruce of a single.

Romo batted for himself and struck out before finishing the Reds from the mound, then discussed the emotion of that 10th inning, when the Giants refused to let their season die.

"Everyone was fired up and saying, 'We can get it done. We've got to do this now,'" Romo said. "We're a high-strung team and we have a lot of energy, and being able to take that to the top of the 10th and get ahead, I mean, that was huge for us."

BOX SCORE

Giants 2, Reds 1 (10)

Giants	AB	R	H	BI	BB	SO	Avg.
Pagan cf	3	0	0	1	0	1	.083
Scutaro 2b	4	0	1	0	0	0	.083
Sandoval 3b	4	0	0	0	0	2	.154
Posey c	4	1	1	0	0	2	.273
Pence rf	4	0	1	0	0	2	.083
Belt 1b	4	0	0	0	0	3	.111
G.Blanco lf	1	1	0	0	0	1	.333
Nady ph-lf	2	0	0	0	0	2	.000
B.Crawford ss	1	0	0	0	1	1	.000
Arias ph-ss	2	0	0	0	0	0	.333
Vogelsong p	0	0	0	0	0	0	—
A.Huff ph	1	0	0	0	0	1	.000
Affeldt p	0	0	0	0	0	0	—
Theriot ph	1	0	0	0	0	0	.000
S.Casilla p	0	0	0	0	0	0	—
Ja.Lopez p	0	0	0	0	0	0	—
Romo p	1	0	0	0	0	1	.000
Totals	32	2	3	1	1	16	

Cincinnati	AB	R	H	BI	BB	SO	Avg.
B.Phillips 2b	5	0	1	0	0	2	.400
Cozart ss	4	1	0	0	1	1	.167
Votto 1b	2	0	0	0	2	0	.333
Ludwick lf	3	0	1	0	1	1	.333
Bruce rf	3	0	1	1	0	0	.333
Rolen 3b	4	0	1	0	0	2	.182
Hanigan c	4	0	0	0	0	0	.250
Stubbs cf	4	0	0	0	0	0	.167
H.Bailey p	2	0	0	0	0	1	.000
Frazier ph	1	0	0	0	0	0	.000
Marshall p	0	0	0	0	0	0	—
A.Chapman p	0	0	0	0	0	0	—
Broxton p	0	0	0	0	0	0	—
Paul ph	1	0	0	0	0	0	.500
Totals	33	1	4	1	4	7	

Giants	001	000	000	1	—	2	3	0
Cincinnati	100	000	000	0	—	1	4	1

E—Rolen (2). **LOB**—Giants 4, Cincinnati 7. **RBIs**—Pagan (1), Bruce (4). **SB**—B.Phillips (1). **S**—Vogelsong. **SF**—Pagan.

Giants	IP	H	R	ER	BB	SO	NP	ERA
Vogelsong	5	3	1	1	3	5	95	1.80
Affeldt	2	1	0	0	0	1	22	0.00
S.Casilla	⅔	0	0	0	1	1	19	4.50
Ja.Lopez	⅓	0	0	0	0	0	1	0.00
Romo W, 1-0	2	0	0	0	0	0	15	0.00

Cincinnati	IP	H	R	ER	BB	SO	NP	ERA
H.Bailey	7	1	1	1	1	10	88	1.29
Marshall	1	0	0	0	0	1	10	0.00
A.Chapman	1	0	0	0	0	2	15	4.50
Broxton L, 0-1	1	2	1	0	0	3	24	0.00

Inherited runners-scored—Ja.Lopez 1-0. **HBP**—by Affeldt (Bruce), by H.Bailey (G.Blanco). **PB**—Hanigan. **Umpires**—Home, Gerry Davis; First, Dan Iassogna; Second, Tom Hallion; Third, Chad Fairchild; Right, Brian O'Nora; Left, Phil Cuzzi. **Time**—3:41. **Attendance**—44,501 (42,319).

NLDS GAME 4

BRING ON

■ BY HENRY SCHULMAN

The progression of Giants moods in this Division Series has been fascinating as it moved from optimism to shock to relief and now defiance.

As Buster Posey stood in the clubhouse after Wednesday's 8-3 victory, which forced a decisive Game 5 that seemed inconceivable after the team's two-game disappearance in San Francisco, he was asked about having to beat archnemesis Mat Latos on Thursday to advance.

"I think we've got a good one going for us, too," Posey said in dismissing the question.

Matt Cain gets the ball with a chance to pitch the Giants to the National League Championship Series, an opportunity they created when the offense rose after three teeth-gnashing games, took advantage

Opposite Page: Gregor Blanco hits a two-run home run in the second inning, as the San Francisco Giants take the lead over the Cincinnati Reds 3-1. *Michael Macor*

Above: The Giants beat the Cincinnati Reds 8-3 to take Game 4 of the National League Division Series. *Michael Macor*

of the Reds' chaotic pitching situation and blasted them out of Great American Ball Park.

Angel Pagan homered off emergency starter Mike Leake to start the game, the first San Francisco or New York Giant to do that in the postseason. Gregor Blanco added a two-run homer off Leake and Pablo Sandoval blasted one 422 feet with a man aboard off reliever Jose Arredondo.

Marco Scutaro, 1-for-14 in the series, hit an RBI double. Joaquin Arias came off the bench and hit two doubles, scoring each time. Sandoval also had a sacrifice fly to finish with three RBIs.

Just as important, Tim Lincecum emerged from the bullpen with two on and two outs in the fourth inning to protect a 3-2 lead and stuck around through the eighth, sparing a bullpen that had worked hard for Tuesday's 10-inning win.

Lincecum gave up two hits and a run in $4^1/_3$ innings. Forty-two of his 55 pitches were strikes.

And it all happened after Hunter Pence again gathered the team in the dugout before the first pitch for a hoorah speech, the way he did before Game 3. He was reticent to talk about it Tuesday but loosened up Wednesday and summarized his feelings.

" 'We will see you tomorrow' is kind of our message," Pence said. "All of us want to play together.

NLDS GAME 4

Above: Giants Pablo Sandoval doubles in the first inning, as the Giants take on the Cincinnati Reds in Game 4 of the National League Division Series in Cincinnati. *Michael Macor*

All of us want to be on the field. This is one of the most fun group of guys, and we enjoy it."

Asked if he will try to ignite the team again before Game 5, Pence said, "I'm pretty sure we'll be doing it again."

Pence said Pagan "kind of charged up there out of the dugout" to face Leake, who was put on the Division Series roster in place of injured Johnny Cueto and given the start.

Pagan homered into the right-field seats to give the Giants the quick lead. The Reds tied it on a bases-loaded walk issued by Barry Zito in the bottom half, but Blanco followed a Hector Sanchez single in the third with a liner into the same bleachers.

Sandoval's homer was no line drive. He crushed it high and deep into the Giants' bullpen in the right-field corner.

"It's just unbelievable. It was so fun to watch," Zito said after the postseason start that eluded him in 2010 did not last three innings. "I went inside to watch a little video then went back out there to cheer the boys on. Pablo's homer was the nail in the coffin."

No, Sandoval said, "The important home run was Pagan's because it woke up our offense."

Zito left with a 3-2 lead in the third, when Bochy donned his mad bullpen scientist hat. George Kontos, a rookie making a big impact, retired Drew Stubbs on a pop foul to end the inning. Kontos got a strikeout but allowed two singles in the fourth before Bochy summoned lefty Jose Mijares to face Joey Votto.

Mijares pumped his fist wildly when he fanned Votto for the second out. Bochy then turned to Lincecum, not to start a clean inning but to preserve a one-run lead with two runners aboard. Bochy created a favorable matchup, though. Ryan Ludwick was 3-for-23 against Lincecum.

Lincecum fell behind 2-0 but recovered to get the strikeout. For the next four innings, he was Cy Young Timmy in walking none and striking out six.

"Getting that strikeout of Ludwick, that was the difference in the game," Zito said. "We just fed off the momentum after that."

The Giants scored twice in the fifth on doubles by Arias and Pagan plus the Sandoval sacrifice fly, then finished Cincinnati with a three-run eighth against Arredondo in another rally that began with an Arias double.

Santiago Casilla pitched the ninth in a win that sets up another do-or-die game. If they win, they will be the first team in major-league history to overcome an 0-2 deficit by taking three straight on the road.

Even if the Giants are eliminated Thursday, they can say they put up a fight.

"I'm not ready for that," Pagan said, "but if it happens, I think we put out our best effort. After two losses in a row we came here to tie it up. We're ready to win tomorrow. We have to get it done."

BOX SCORE

Giants 8, Reds 3

Giants	AB	R	H	BI	BB	SO	Avg.
Pagan cf	3	2	2	2	2	0	.200
Scutaro 2b	4	1	1	1	0	0	.125
Sandoval 3b	4	1	3	3	0	0	.294
Posey 1b	4	0	0	0	1	0	.200
Belt 1b	0	0	0	0	0	0	.111
Pence rf	4	0	1	0	0	1	.125
H.Sanchez c	2	1	1	0	2	1	.500
G.Blanco lf	4	1	1	2	0	2	.300
B.Crawford ss	2	0	0	0	0	0	.000
Lincecum p	2	0	0	0	0	1	.000
S.Casilla p	0	0	0	0	0	0	—
Zito p	1	0	0	0	0	0	.000
Kontos p	0	0	0	0	0	0	—
Mijares p	0	0	0	0	0	0	—
Arias ss	3	2	2	0	0	1	.500
Totals	**33**	**8**	**11**	**8**	**5**	**6**	

Cincinnati	AB	R	H	BI	BB	SO	Avg.
B.Phillips 2b	4	0	1	1	0	2	.368
Cozart ss	5	0	2	0	0	0	.235
Votto 1b	5	1	2	0	0	2	.357
Ludwick lf	4	1	1	1	1	1	.308
Bruce rf	3	0	0	0	1	1	.267
Frazier 3b	3	0	1	1	0	2	.000
D.Navarro c	3	0	1	0	1	2	.333
Stubbs cf	4	1	1	0	0	1	.188
Leake p	2	0	1	0	0	1	.500
LeCure p	0	0	0	0	0	0	—
Cairo ph	1	0	0	0	0	0	.000
Arredondo p	0	0	0	0	0	0	—
Hoover p	0	0	0	0	0	0	—
Heisey ph	1	0	0	0	0	1	.000
Simon p	0	0	0	0	0	0	—
Totals	**35**	**3**	**9**	**3**	**4**	**13**	

Giants	120	020	300	—	8 11 1
Cincinnati	101	001	000	—	3 9 0

E—Lincecum (1). **LOB**—Giants 5, Cincinnati 10. **2B**—Pagan (1), Scutaro (1), Sandoval (2), Arias 2 (2), Stubbs (1). **HR**—Pagan (1), off Leake; G.Blanco (1), off Leake; Sandoval (1), off Arredondo; Ludwick (2), off Zito. **RBIs**—Pagan 2 (3), Scutaro (1), Sandoval 3 (3), G.Blanco 2 (2), B.Phillips (5), Ludwick (2), Frazier (1). **CS**—Pagan (1). **S**—Scutaro. **SF**—Sandoval, B.Phillips. **Runners moved up**—Pagan, Posey, Cairo. **GIDP**—Pence, Lincecum. **DP**—Cincinnati 2 (B.Phillips, Cozart, Votto), (Frazier, Cozart, Votto).

Giants	IP	H	R	ER	BB	SO	NP	ERA
Zito	2⅔	4	2	2	4	4	76	6.75
Kontos	⅔	2	0	0	0	1	9	0.00
Mijares	⅓	0	0	0	0	1	5	81.00
Lincecum W, 1-0	4⅓	2	1	1	0	6	55	1.42
S.Casilla	1	1	0	0	0	1	25	3.00

Cincinnati	IP	H	R	ER	BB	SO	NP	ERA
Leake L, 0-1	4⅓	6	5	5	2	1	71	10.38
LeCure	1⅔	1	0	0	0	3	20	0.00
Arredondo	⅓	3	3	3	1	0	19	20.25
Hoover	1⅔	0	0	0	1	1	15	0.00
Simon	1	1	0	0	1	1	22	0.00

Inherited runners-scored—Kontos 1-0, Mijares 2-0, Lincecum 2-0, LeCure 1-1, Hoover 1-0. **Umpires**—Home, Dan Iassogna; First, Tom Hallion; Second, Chad Fairchild; Third, Phil Cuzzi; Right, Gerry Davis; Left, Brian O'Nora. **Time**—3:35. **Attendance**—44,375 (42,319).

NLDS GAME 5

GIANTS HISTORIC SERIES COMEBACK COMPLETE, THEY HEAD TO NLCS

BY HENRY SCHULMAN

With bedlam in the clubhouse surrounding him, as loud and bubbly as these things get, Sergio Romo stood alone, his back to a locker, and tried desperately not to cry.

He was winning the battle until he was asked what filled his mind during his riveting and spectacular 12-pitch duel with Jay Bruce in the ninth inning, as the Giants' season teetered in the balance. He choked up, and his eyes glistened.

"I was thinking about my teammates," Romo said." I couldn't let them down. It was not in me. Holy cow, I couldn't let them down."

It was a battle that Romo won. He got Bruce on a fly to left, then struck out Scott Rolen to save a 6-4 victory that sealed the Giants' historic comeback in their Division Series against the Reds. It also made Buster Posey's fifth-inning grand slam against Mat Latos stand up as one of the most important homers in franchise history.

The Giants preserved their hopes of winning a second World Series in three years and advanced to the National League Championship Series as the first team to win a five-game postseason series by losing twice at home and then winning three potential elimination games on the road.

They will play the winner of Friday night's Game 5 between the Nationals and Cardinals. If Washington wins, the NLCS will begin there. If St. Louis wins, Games 1 and 2 will be played at AT&T Park. Either way, the first game is Sunday.

Posey's grand slam, the third in franchise post-

Above: Giants starting pitcher Matt Cain throws in the first inning as the Giants take on the Reds in Game 5 of the National League Division Series in Cincinnati. *Michael Macor*

Above: Hunter Pence, Marco Scutaro, Angel Pagan, Gregor Blanco and Xavier Nady celebrate as the Giants beat the Reds 6-4 in game five to win the National League Division Series in Cincinnati. *Michael Marcor*

season history, capped a six-run fifth inning that gave the Giants a 6-0 lead. Matt Cain and five relievers then stopped a furious Cincinnati comeback.

Before each of the games at Great American Ball Park, Hunter Pence implored his teammates in the dugout to fight every moment so they could keep their season alive.

"They don't want to go home," general manager Brian Sabean said. "It's like the 2010 team. It's pretty amazing. They love to be around each other."

Posey placed this series win "probably right behind winning the World Series," but begged to differ with his GM in one regard.

"In 2010, we were never down in a series," Posey said. "It was really a different feeling to me to know it was time to get something done or we're going home."

Injured closer Brian Wilson described the feeling in his unique way after he watched his replacement complete a save that will live prominently in Giants lore.

"To be honest with you, I was screaming and going nuts all game," Wilson said. "I could puke right now, and I've got a raging headache, and I wouldn't change a damn thing."

Cain beat the Reds for the first time in four games this season, including Game 1 of the Division

NATIONAL LEAGUE DIVISION SERIES GAME 5   73

Above: Giants manager Bruce Bochy watches in the eighth inning, as the Giants went on to beat the Reds 6-4 in Game 5 to win the National League Division Series in Cincinnati. *Michael Macor*

Series. The Giants beat Latos for the first time in 2012 after he and Cain engaged for four innings in a scoreless duel expected from two pitchers of that caliber in a deciding game.

Gregor Blanco ignited the rally that broke the deadlock, grounding a single through the left side to start the fifth. Brandon Crawford then tripled into the right-field corner, his first hit of the series, to produce the game's first run.

With one out, the Giants got a huge break when Angel Pagan hit a high chopper to the left side of a drawn-in infield. Shortstop Zack Cozart had a play at home and rushed as he leaped to field the ball. He dropped it for an error, Crawford scoring for a 2-0 lead and Pagan reaching first.

Latos then walked Marco Scutaro before Pablo Sandoval singled for the second time to load the bases, setting up the Latos-Posey matchup. Posey already had two homers against the right-hander, one at San Diego when Latos was a Padre, one on Saturday.

Posey got ahead 2-1 but chased a fastball away. When Latos threw a 2-2 sinker, Posey crushed it 434 feet, just above the facing of the second deck in left. As the ball floated back toward the first deck, the Giants went berserk in the dugout. Posey had his second career slam, and the Giants had a 6-0 lead.

"I was fortunate to get the barrel on it and hit it hard," Posey said in his usual understated way. "I didn't do much the whole series. I probably was a little overanxious at times. I was happy to be in that situation. I think any guy in the lineup wants to be in that spot. I was fortunate to get the job done."

His teammates were much less reserved. Pagan said someone popped him in the jaw during the dugout celebration, and he "wobbled a little bit."

Then, the Giants' pitching wobbled a little bit.

The Reds got two back on a Brandon Phillips double in the bottom of the inning. Ryan Ludwick's second homer of the series against Cain, leading off the sixth, made it 6-3.

74 SAN FRANCISCO GIANTS: A RETURN TO THE PINNACLE

Then, the pitching staff went into survival mode. Cain and Posey executed a strike-'em-out, throw-'em-out double play later in the inning. That ended Cain's day.

George Kontos got the final out of the sixth. Jeremy Affeldt stranded two with a Ludwick comebacker in the seventh. Romo stranded two more in the eighth when Pagan made a diving catch to rob pinch-hitter Dioner Navarro, the second big play of the inning. Crawford prevented a Ryan Hanigan single with a diving backhanded catch.

Romo retook the mound in the ninth with a 6-3 lead. He got Phillips to pop out but walked Cozart. Singles by Joey Votto and Ludwick produced a run and put the tying runs on base. Bruce stepped in as the potential winning run with 34 regular-season homers on his resume, a left-handed hitter.

Jose Mijares was warming in the bullpen, but manager Bruce Bochy was not going there.

"If we were going to go down," Bochy said, "Romo was going to be on the mound."

The encounter was epic, the crowd of 44,142 making as much noise as they could.

Bruce fouled off six consecutive 1-2 pitches and built the count to 3-2. Romo had thrown only one slider in the first 11 pitches. The rest were fastballs, aside from one changeup. With the count full, Romo went with the backdoor slider, a decision that Posey said took "guts" because a hanging slider might have flown 500 feet and ended the Giants' season.

"He was committed to that pitch," Posey said. "It was one of the best battles I've ever been a part of, because of the situation that we were in. Romo kept on executing, and Jay kept on fighting off some tough pitches."

When the slider reached the plate, Bruce hit it harmlessly to left for the out. The Rolen strikeout was no less critical, but it seemed anticlimactic. Strike three was another backdoor slider.

"If I was going to lose, I was going to lose with my best pitch," Romo said. "I always knew I was going to win that battle. There was never a doubt in my mind."

BOX SCORE

Giants 6, Reds 4

Giants	AB	R	H	BI	BB	SO	Avg.
Pagan cf	5	1	0	1	0	1	.150
Scutaro 2b	4	1	1	0	1	0	.150
Sandoval 3b	4	1	2	0	0	0	.333
Arias 3b	0	0	0	0	0	0	.500
Posey c	4	1	1	4	0	0	.211
Pence rf	4	0	2	0	0	0	.200
Belt 1b	4	0	0	0	0	3	.077
G.Blanco lf	4	1	1	0	0	0	.286
Romo p	0	0	0	0	0	0	.000
B.Crawford ss	4	1	2	1	0	1	.182
M.Cain p	3	0	0	0	0	2	.000
Kontos p	0	0	0	0	0	0	—
Affeldt p	0	0	0	0	0	0	—
Ja.Lopez p	0	0	0	0	0	0	—
S.Casilla p	0	0	0	0	0	0	—
Nady lf	1	0	0	0	0	0	.000
Totals	**37**	**6**	**9**	**6**	**1**	**7**	

Cincinnati	AB	R	H	BI	BB	SO	Avg.
B.Phillips 2b	5	0	2	2	0	0	.375
Cozart ss	4	1	1	0	1	0	.238
Votto 1b	4	0	2	0	1	1	.389
Ludwick lf	5	1	2	2	0	1	.333
Bruce rf	4	0	1	0	1	1	.263
Rolen 3b	5	0	2	0	0	1	.250
Hanigan c	3	1	0	0	0	1	.200
Stubbs cf	3	1	1	0	0	1	.211
Frazier ph	1	0	1	0	0	0	.167
W.Valdez cf	0	0	0	0	0	0	.000
Latos p	1	0	0	0	0	0	.000
LeCure p	0	0	0	0	0	0	—
Heisey ph	1	0	0	0	0	0	.000
Marshall p	0	0	0	0	0	0	—
Paul ph	1	0	0	0	0	1	.333
Broxton p	0	0	0	0	0	0	—
D.Navarro ph	1	0	0	0	0	0	.250
A.Chapman p	0	0	0	0	0	0	—
Totals	**38**	**4**	**12**	**4**	**3**	**7**	

Giants	000	060	000	—	6	9	1
Cincinnati	000	021	001	—	4	12	1

E—Sandoval (1), Cozart (1). **LOB**—Giants 5, Cincinnati 11. **2B**—B.Phillips (3). **3B**—B.Crawford (1). **HR**—Posey (2), off Latos; Ludwick (3), off M.Cain. **RBIs**—Pagan (4), Posey 4 (5), B.Crawford (1), B.Phillips 2 (7), Ludwick 2 (4). **SB**—Pence (1). **CS**—Bruce (1). **Runners moved up**—Belt. **GIDP**—Hanigan. **DP**—Giants 2 (B.Crawford, Scutaro, Belt), (Posey, Posey, Sandoval).

Giants	IP	H	R	ER	BB	SO	NP	ERA
M.Cain W, 1-1	5⅔	6	3	3	2	5	96	5.06
Kontos H, 1	⅓	0	0	0	0	0	2	0.00
Affeldt H, 1	1	2	0	0	0	1	24	0.00
Ja.Lopez H, 1	⅓	0	0	0	0	0	4	0.00
S.Casilla H, 1	⅓	2	0	0	0	0	12	2.70
Romo S, 1-1	1⅓	2	1	1	1	1	35	2.08

Cincinnati	IP	H	R	ER	BB	SO	NP	ERA
Latos L, 0-1	4⅓	7	6	5	1	4	79	6.48
LeCure	⅔	0	0	0	0	1	8	0.00
Marshall	2	0	0	0	0	2	17	0.00
Broxton	1	1	0	0	0	0	15	0.00
A.Chapman	1	1	0	0	0	1	25	3.00

Inherited runners-scored—Kontos 1-0, Romo 2-0. **HBP**—by M.Cain (Hanigan). **Umpires**—Home, Tom Hallion; First, Chad Fairchild; Second, Phil Cuzzi; Third, Brian O'Nora; Right, Dan Iassogna; Left, Gerry Davis. **Time**—3:52. **Attendance**—44,142 (42,319).

NLCS GAME 1

THE HOME-FIELD DISADVANTAGE

■ BY HENRY SCHULMAN

So, Giants, is this how it's going to be until the final out of the 2012 postseason, doing everything the hard way? Falling behind early in games and series? Getting little from the starting pitchers? Sending more than 42,000 fans home from AT&T Park disappointed every time?

This is not a blueprint for success, but a way to ensure that another team will enjoy a parade in early November. It worked for the Giants in their Division Series against the Reds. Now, against the Cardinals, the Giants are playing with fire.

They dropped Game 1 of the National League Championship Series 6-4 Sunday night by continuing two trends that they somehow survived in the last round: Their starter was pounded and the Giants lost at home.

Madison Bumgarner allowed six runs before his fourth-inning exit. The Giants charged back with four in the bottom half but got skunked the rest of the way.

The Giants have played six games in this postseason, winning the three on the road and losing three at home. Since 1962, they have played 37 postseason games in San Francisco and had only one other three-game losing streak, the final two games of the 1989 World Series against the A's and Game 3 of the 1997 Division Series against the Marlins. That trend by definition has to change for the Giants to advance to the World Series. They have to win at least once at China Basin.

"We can't get ourselves behind the 8-ball like we did last time and try to fight back on the road again, " Ryan Vogelsong said." It was tremendous we did it once, and I think it would be asking a lot of us to do it again.

"I'm not saying we couldn't do it if it happens, but I think it's important for us to (win) here." Vogelsong, who pitches Game 2 against Chris Carpenter on Monday, stands out in this postseason because he had a good start, holding the Reds to one run over five innings in Game 3 of the Division Series.

Above: Giants third baseman Pablo Sandoval strikes out in the fourth inning during Game 1 in San Francisco. *Brant Ward*

76 SAN FRANCISCO GIANTS: A RETURN TO THE PINNACLE

Above: Madison Bumgarner (right) stood on the mound after giving up a home run to David Freese. *Brant Ward*

Overall, the rotation has allowed 19 earned runs over 30 1/3 innings, a 5.64 ERA. No starter has finished six innings.

"I think it's a little surprising," catcher Buster Posey said, "but it's not something we can't fix." One fix might be yanking Bumgarner from his potential Game 5 start, a notion that would have seemed ridiculous before the playoffs, but less so after the Reds and Cardinals battered him for 10 runs in eight innings.

"He's one of our guys," manager Bruce Bochy said. "He's had a great year and we've seen what this kid's done for us during the season and in the postseason. But it is something we'll discuss." Bumgarner normally throws his fastball about 92 mph. He is now at 89. He said he feels strong, but perhaps all the innings he threw this year and in the past three years are taking a toll.

Asked about his stuff Sunday, he said, "Not very good. That's the way it's been the past five starts. There's not a whole lot of life on the ball."

Tim Lincecum again threw his hat into the ring for a start with two hitless relief innings. In three games out of the bullpen, he has allowed one run in 8 1/3 innings. Bochy said Lincecum is in the mix for Game 4.

Bumgarner's 11-pitch first inning offered hope for the lefty. David Freese's two-run homer in the second inning tempered it. In the fourth, it was squashed. With two runs already in, Bumgarner

NATIONAL LEAGUE CHAMPIONSHIP SERIES GAME 1

NLCS GAME 1

Above: The Giants watch the eighth inning from the dugout down 6-4 during Game 1 of the NLCS at AT&T Park. *Michael Macor*

threw a hit-me fastball to Carlos Beltran, who hit it into the left-field bleachers for a 6-0 St. Louis lead. Bumgarner allowed five homers in 106 regular-season innings at AT&T Park. In eight postseason innings, he has surrendered three.

Unlike his Game 2 start in the Division Series, when the Giants played dead and fell 9-0, they stormed back against Lance Lynn after Marco Scutaro's leadoff single in the fourth.

With two outs, Hunter Pence singled ahead of three scoring hits, a Brandon Belt single, Gregor Blanco's two-run triple and Brandon Crawford's double, which cut St. Louis' lead to 6-4 and revived a sullen crowd.

Second baseman Daniel Descalso's diving stop of Angel Pagan's grounder prevented a fifth run, and the Giants did not threaten again.

Six relievers blanked the Giants on two hits. Blanco called the Giants' futility at AT&T Park "a little weird." Pagan said it's just a matter of being outplayed at the wrong time.

"We wish we could give (the fans) the victory they're looking for," Pagan said. "The Cardinals just put better at-bats than us and went up 6-0. That's a pretty good lead in the playoffs. It's hard to battle back."

BOX SCORE

Cardinals 6, Giants 4

St. Louis	AB	R	H	BI	BB	SO	Avg.
Jay cf	5	1	1	1	0	1	.200
Beltran rf	4	1	1	2	0	0	.250
Holliday lf	4	0	1	0	0	0	.250
Craig 1b	3	0	0	0	1	1	.000
Y.Molina c	4	1	1	0	0	1	.250
Freese 3b	4	1	1	2	0	1	.250
Descalso 2b	4	1	2	0	0	1	.500
Kozma ss	4	1	1	1	0	1	.250
Lynn p	1	0	0	0	1	1	.000
J.Kelly p	0	0	0	0	0	0	—
Rzepczynski p	0	0	0	0	0	0	—
Schumaker ph	1	0	0	0	0	0	.000
Rosenthal p	0	0	0	0	0	0	—
Mujica p	0	0	0	0	0	0	—
Boggs p	0	0	0	0	0	0	—
S.Robinson ph	1	0	0	0	0	0	.000
Motte p	0	0	0	0	0	0	—
Totals	35	6	8	6	2	7	

Giants	AB	R	H	BI	BB	SO	Avg.
Pagan cf	5	0	1	0	0	1	.200
Scutaro 2b	5	1	2	0	0	1	.400
Sandoval 3b	3	0	0	0	1	2	.000
Posey c	3	0	0	0	1	1	.000
Pence rf	4	1	1	0	0	0	.250
Belt 1b	4	1	1	1	0	0	.250
G.Blanco lf	4	1	1	2	0	0	.250
B.Crawford ss	4	0	1	1	0	1	.250
Bumgarner p	1	0	0	0	0	1	.000
Kontos p	0	0	0	0	0	0	—
A.Huff ph	0	0	0	0	1	0	—
Lincecum p	0	0	0	0	0	0	—
Theriot ph	0	0	0	0	1	0	—
Affeldt p	0	0	0	0	0	0	—
S.Casilla p	0	0	0	0	0	0	—
Mijares p	0	0	0	0	0	0	—
H.Sanchez ph	1	0	0	0	0	0	.000
Totals	34	4	7	4	4	7	

St.Louis	020	400	000	—	6	8	0
Giants	000	400	000	—	4	7	1

E—Sandoval (1). **LOB**—St. Louis 4, Giants 7. **2B**—Descalso (1), Kozma (1), B.Crawford (1). **3B**—G.Blanco (1). **HR**—Freese (1), off Bumgarner; Beltran (1), off Bumgarner. **RBIs**—Jay (1), Beltran 2 (2), Freese 2 (2), Kozma (1), Belt (1), G.Blanco 2 (2), B.Crawford (1). **SB**—Holliday (1), Kozma (1). **Runners moved up**—Sandoval. **GIDP**—Freese. **DP**—Giants 1 (Scutaro, B.Crawford, Belt).

St. Louis	IP	H	R	ER	BB	SO	NP	ERA
Lynn	3⅔	5	4	4	2	3	85	9.82
J.Kelly	1	1	0	0	1	0	13	0.00
Rzepczynski	⅓	0	0	0	0	0	3	0.00
Rosenthal H, 1	1	0	0	0	1	1	16	0.00
Mujica W, 1-0 H, 1	1	0	0	0	0	3	13	0.00
Boggs H, 1	1	0	0	0	0	0	10	0.00
Motte S, 1-1	1	1	0	0	0	0	17	0.00

Giants	IP	H	R	ER	BB	SO	NP	ERA
Bumgarner L, 0-1	3⅔	8	6	6	1	2	73	14.73
Kontos	⅓	0	0	0	0	0	2	0.00
Lincecum	2	0	0	0	1	1	24	0.00
Affeldt	1	0	0	0	0	0	8	0.00
S.Casilla	1	0	0	0	0	2	19	0.00
Mijares	1	0	0	0	2	2	12	0.00

Inherited runners-scored—J.Kelly 2-0, Rzepczynski 2-0. **Umpires**—Home, Gary Darling; First, Chris Guccione; Second, Bill Miller; Third, Greg Gibson; Right, Jerry Layne; Left, Ted Barrett. **Time**—3:21. **Attendance**—42,534 (41,915).

NATIONAL LEAGUE CHAMPIONSHIP SERIES GAME 1

NLCS GAME 2

SCUTARO EVENS THE SCORE

BY HENRY SCHULMAN

Hunter Pence could preach until he was hoarse. He could build a pulpit aside the water jug in the dugout and beg for togetherness and fight until the seagulls arrived for their nightly prowl at AT&T Park.

None of that would fire up the Giants more than the sight of Cardinals left fielder Matt Holliday barreling over second base and crashing into Marco Scutaro's legs as Holliday broke up a first-inning double play, sending the diminutive second baseman writhing on the ground with a hip injury.

How intriguing that an opponent would give the Giants the spark they needed to capture their first home game of this postseason, a 7-1 victory that sent the National League Championship Series to St. Louis at one win apiece.

How inspiring for the Giants that the aggrieved became the aggressor. Scutaro stayed in the game long enough to hit a two-out, bases-loaded single off Chris Carpenter in the fourth inning that scored two. As Scutaro rounded first base, he could see Holliday boot the ball to let a third run score for a 5-1 lead.

Scutaro was smarting when he hit it. He left the game in the sixth when the pain in his left hip became too great. X-rays were negative. Scutaro will undergo an MRI exam Tuesday morning before the Giants fly to St. Louis.

"We're hoping for the best," manager Bruce Bochy said before he criticized Holliday's slide. "I really think they got away with an illegal slide

Above: Giants shortstop Brandon Crawford thows out Cardinals catcher Yadier Molina to end the top of the first inning. *Beck Diefenbach*

80 SAN FRANCISCO GIANTS: A RETURN TO THE PINNACLE

Above: Giants left fielder Gregor Blanco is called safe at first base in the eighth inning at AT&T Park in San Francisco.
Beck Diefenbach

there," Bochy said." He really didn't hit the dirt until he was past the bag. That rule was changed a while back. Marco was behind the bag and got smoked. It's a shame somebody got hurt because of this. He got hit pretty good, and that's a big guy running."

The way Scutaro rolled in the dirt, it was easy to imagine his postseason being over. But he kept playing.

Brandon Crawford, who threw the ball after fielding Allen Craig's slow chopper, was asked if he was surprised Scutaro was able to get the big hit later. "I was surprised he got off a throw to first," Crawford said. "He's a tough player."

The Giants retaliated for Holliday's takeout not by plunking him but by sticking pitcher Chris Carpenter for five runs (two earned).

Angel Pagan hit Carpenter's fourth pitch into the Arcade to join Jimmy Rollins as the only players in postseason history with two game-opening homers in a single postseason.

Brandon Belt hit a bloop double off the tip of his bat to start the four-run fourth and scored on a Carpenter throwing error before the Giants loaded the bases for Scutaro.

In one final jab at the Cardinals, Ryan Theriot, who replaced Scutaro, hit a two-run single in the eighth inning.

The Giants also got their first start of at least six innings in the postseason. Ryan Vogelsong went

NATIONAL LEAGUE CHAMPIONSHIP SERIES GAME 2

NLCS GAME 2

Above: Cardinals left fielder Matt Holliday slides into Giants second baseman Marco Scutaro in the first inning during Game 2 of the NLCS at AT&T Park in San Francisco. *Beck Diefenbach*

seven innings and held the Cardinals to one run on four hits, getting his first postseason win against a pitcher who has 10.

Vogelsong has been the rotation's savior in the playoffs, allowing two earned runs over 12 innings. Matt Cain, Madison Bumgarner and Barry Zito together have given up 18 earned runs in 21 1/3. The Giants also broke their home-field hex.

"Hopefully that gives us some confidence," Buster Posey said, "but I'd love to go to St. Louis and win the next three and not play here until the next round."

Giants players agreed with Bochy that Holliday's charge over the bag was late and uncalled for, but they stopped short of calling it dirty. They used the word "frustrated" more than "angry" and expressed more concern for their second baseman than enmity toward Holliday.

"I was angry, but not because I thought it was dirty," Pagan said. "You get angry when you lose a player like Scutaro. He's a huge piece of the puzzle. You don't want to lose a guy like him. I'm praying he's OK."

Jeremy Affeldt said Holliday, a former teammate, had an anguished look on his face after the play. Holliday defended himself and expressed remorse at the same time.

"I'm not a dirty player," he said. "I was just trying to keep us out of the double play. I hope he's OK. He's a good guy. I told Buster to tell Marco I wish I started my slide earlier, and obviously I wasn't trying to hurt him."

Perhaps the clubhouse attitude would have been harsher had Scutaro been carted off. Instead, he took the swing that propelled the Giants to a badly needed win.

Nobody was more motivated by Scutaro than the Great Motivator.

"This is playoff baseball," Pence said. "You have to earn everything. I don't think Holliday wanted to go out and hurt him. Seeing Marco stay in the game and do what he did was inspiring."

BOX SCORE

Giants 7, Cardinals 1

St. Louis	AB	R	H	BI	BB	SO	Avg.
Jay cf	4	0	0	0	0	0	.111
Beltran rf	3	0	2	0	1	0	.429
Holliday lf	4	0	1	0	0	0	.250
Craig 1b	3	0	0	0	0	1	.000
Y.Molina c	4	0	1	0	0	0	.250
Freese 3b	4	0	0	0	0	0	.125
Descalso 2b	4	0	0	0	0	1	.250
Kozma ss	3	1	0	0	1	2	.143
C.Carpenter p	1	0	1	1	0	0	1.000
Schumaker ph	1	0	0	0	0	1	.000
J.Kelly p	0	0	0	0	0	0	—
Salas p	0	0	0	0	0	0	—
Chambers ph	1	0	0	0	0	0	.000
S.Miller p	0	0	0	0	0	0	—
Rzepczynski p	0	0	0	0	0	0	—
Totals	32	1	5	1	2	5	

Giants	AB	R	H	BI	BB	SO	Avg.
Pagan cf	4	2	2	1	1	0	.333
Scutaro 2b	3	0	2	2	0	0	.500
Theriot 2b	2	0	1	2	0	0	.500
Sandoval 3b	5	0	1	0	0	1	.125
Posey c	5	0	1	0	0	2	.125
Pence rf	3	0	0	0	1	0	.143
Belt 1b	4	1	2	0	0	1	.375
G.Blanco lf	3	2	1	0	1	0	.286
B.Crawford ss	4	1	0	1	0	0	.125
Vogelsong p	2	0	1	0	0	1	.500
Affeldt p	0	0	0	0	0	0	—
A.Huff ph	1	1	1	0	0	0	1.000
Romo p	0	0	0	0	0	0	—
Totals	36	7	12	6	3	5	

St.Louis	010	000	000	—	1	5	2
Giants	100	400	02x	—	7	12	0

E—C.Carpenter (1), Holliday (1). **LOB**—St. Louis 7, Giants 9. **2B**—Beltran 2 (2), C.Carpenter (1), Belt (1), Vogelsong (1). **HR**—Pagan (1), off C.Carpenter. **RBIs**—C.Carpenter (1), Pagan (1), Scutaro 2 (2), Theriot 2 (2), B.Crawford (2). **S**—Vogelsong.

St. Louis	IP	H	R	ER	BB	SO	NP	ERA
C.Carpenter L, 0-1	4	6	5	2	2	1	76	4.50
J.Kelly	1	2	0	0	0	0	17	0.00
Salas	1	1	0	0	0	1	10	0.00
S.Miller	1 1/3	3	2	2	1	2	37	13.50
Rzepczynski	2/3	0	0	0	0	1	5	0.00

Giants	IP	H	R	ER	BB	SO	NP	ERA
Vogelsong W, 1-0	7	4	1	1	2	4	106	1.29
Affeldt	1	0	0	0	0	0	8	0.00
Romo	1	1	0	0	0	1	11	0.00

Inherited runners-scored—Rzepczynski 2-0. **HBP**—by Vogelsong (Craig). **Umpires**—Home, Chris Guccione; First, Bill Miller; Second, Greg Gibson; Third, Ted Barrett; Right, Gary Darling; Left, Jerry Layne. **Time**—3:10. **Attendance**—42,679 (41,915).

NLCS GAME 3

A STUDY IN FRUSTRATION

■ BY HENRY SCHULMAN

A team clinches its division or wins a playoff series, and the players hoot and holler in unfettered joy. Every ounce of their being wants to celebrate and savor. In these giddy moments, they cannot fathom that the next round might bring a day and night of misery like the Giants had at Busch Stadium on Wednesday.

In a 3-1 loss that left them down two games to one in the National League Championship Series, the Giants had so many frustrations that they would be hard-pressed to choose the worst.

Was it a 3-hour, 28-minute rain delay that lasted 26 minutes longer than the game itself? Or landing 12 runners on base in 5 2/3 innings against the Cardi-

84 SAN FRANCISCO GIANTS: A RETURN TO THE PINNACLE

Opposite Page: Giants Marco Scutaro can't stop the Cardinals' Pete Kozma from turning a double play on a ball hit by Pablo Sandoval in the fifth inning. *Michael Macor*

Above: The grounds crew rolls out the tarp during a rain delay in the seventh inning of Game 3 of the National League Championship Series in St. Louis. *Michael Macor*

nals' top starter and scoring once? Or having one of the greatest postseason hitters of all time limp off with a knee injury after one at-bat and losing because his replacement hits a two-run homer?

That was the Giants' story. Now, they will try to write a better one and even the series Thursday behind Tim Lincecum, who will get his first start of the 2012 postseason in a game the Giants sorely need. Otherwise, their season could end before they can bring the NLCS back to San Francisco.

"We're in their home," Angel Pagan said. "They play great over here. We don't want to be behind here, but we've been there before."

The Giants' fourth loss of this postseason was different from the others. For the first time, they wasted a solid start. Matt Cain allowed three runs in $6^2/_3$ innings with the best stuff and command he has had in three playoff games.

The difference in the game was a hanging slider in the third inning that Matt Carpenter sent over the right-field wall for a two-run homer, the rookie's fifth hit in five at-bats against Cain.

Fans in San Francisco need not be embarrassed about not recognizing the name. Carpenter is a role player who did not start the game, but entered after Carlos Beltran wrenched his left knee running out a first-inning groundball.

Beltran has more career home runs per postseason at-bat than Babe Ruth. Beltran leaves the game and Cain gets whacked by his backup.

"With Carlos being out, that's something you

NATIONAL LEAGUE CHAMPIONSHIP SERIES GAME 3

NLCS GAME 3

Above: The Cardinals celebrate after defeating the Giants 3-1 in Game 3 of the National League Championship Series at Busch Stadium in St. Louis. *Carlos Avila Gonzalez*

want to take advantage of," Cain said. "I didn't do a good job of it."

The long ball has been Cain's bane in the playoffs. Carpenter's was the fourth he had given up in a span of $13\tfrac{1}{3}$ innings. In contrast, Cain allowed one homer in $32\tfrac{1}{3}$ innings over his final five regular-season starts.

Carpenter's homer was enough to overcome all the damage the Giants did against Kyle Lohse and four St. Louis relievers. They scored their run in the third inning when Pagan singled, Marco Scutaro doubled and Pablo Sandoval grounded out.

Lohse then walked Buster Posey intentionally to face Hunter Pence, who did exactly what the Car-

86 SAN FRANCISCO GIANTS: A RETURN TO THE PINNACLE

dinals had hoped and ended the inning with a double play, stranding Scutaro at third.

Pence also struck out with two aboard in the seventh against Mitchell Boggs. He is hitting .161 in the postseason with no RBIs in eight games. The great motivator could be lowered in the lineup for Game 4 because he is providing zero protection for Posey.

"I'm the goat today," Pence said. "I didn't get the job done in big opportunities. I'm going to go home, learn from this, and tomorrow I'm going to come back and be hungry."

"He is definitely not the goat," Posey responded when he heard Pence's quote. "I know I feel confident every time he goes up there with guys in scoring position. It's never one guy. We had other opportunities."

The Cards scored their final run in the seventh on a bases-loaded grounder to Scutaro, who had trouble gripping the ball and probably had no play at the plate. He threw to first to get the sure out.

As Bochy emerged to pull Cain, a storm that had threatened downtown St. Louis all day arrived. The tarp came out, the sky turned black, and sheets of rain drenched the 45,850 fans before they took cover.

Down 3-1, the Giants surely did not enjoy the downtime as much as the Cardinals did. Fans always wonder what players do during these long delays. Posey provided a glimpse.

"A lot of sitting," he said. "I walked to the kitchen, I walked to the training room, I walked to the bathroom, then I sat some more."

After all the sitting, six Giants hitters had to face fire-throwing closer Jason Motte. He retired all of them, in order, ending a game that made the Giants' Champagne party in Cincinnati seem so long ago.

BOX SCORE

Cardinals 3, Giants 1

Giants	AB	R	H	BI	BB	SO	Avg.
Pagan cf	5	1	1	0	0	1	.286
Scutaro 2b	5	0	2	0	0	0	.462
Sandoval 3b	5	0	2	1	0	0	.231
Posey c	2	0	1	0	2	0	.200
Pence rf	4	0	0	0	0	1	.091
Belt 1b	3	0	0	0	1	1	.273
G.Blanco lf	3	0	0	0	1	0	.200
B.Crawford ss	3	0	2	0	1	0	.273
M.Cain p	2	0	1	0	0	1	.500
Ja.Lopez p	0	0	0	0	0	0	—
A.Huff ph	1	0	0	0	0	0	.500
Mijares p	0	0	0	0	0	0	—
Kontos p	0	0	0	0	0	0	—
Totals	33	1	9	1	5	4	

St. Louis	AB	R	H	BI	BB	SO	Avg.
Jay cf	3	1	1	0	0	0	.167
Beltran rf	1	0	0	0	0	0	.375
M.Carpenter rf-1b	3	1	1	2	0	1	.333
Holliday lf	4	0	0	0	0	1	.167
Craig 1b	3	0	0	0	0	1	.000
Boggs p	0	0	0	0	0	0	—
Chambers rf	0	0	0	0	1	0	.000
Y.Molina c	4	0	1	0	0	0	.250
Freese 3b	3	1	2	0	0	0	.273
Descalso 2b	2	0	0	0	1	0	.200
Kozma ss	3	0	1	0	0	0	.200
Lohse p	2	0	0	0	0	0	.000
Rosenthal p	0	0	0	0	0	0	—
Mujica p	0	0	0	0	0	0	—
S.Robinson rf	1	0	0	1	0	0	.000
Motte p	0	0	0	0	0	0	—
Totals	29	3	6	3	2	3	

Giants	001	000	000	—	1	9	1
St. Louis	002	000	10x	—	3	6	0

E—M.Cain (1). **LOB**—Giants 11, St. Louis 5. **2B**—Scutaro (1), Freese (1). **HR**—M.Carpenter (1), off M.Cain. **RBIs**—Sandoval (1), M.Carpenter 2 (2), S.Robinson. **S**—M.Cain. **Runners moved up**—Sandoval, G.Blanco, S.Robinson. **GIDP**—Sandoval, Pence, Beltran. **DP**—Giants 1 (Scutaro, B.Crawford, Belt); St. Louis 2 (Kozma, Descalso, Craig), (Descalso, Kozma, Craig).

Giants	IP	H	R	ER	BB	SO	NP	ERA
M.Cain L, 0-1	6⅔	6	3	3	1	2	100	4.05
Ja.Lopez	⅓	0	0	0	0	0	5	0.00
Mijares	⅔	0	0	0	1	1	12	0.00
Kontos	⅓	0	0	0	0	0	5	0.00

St. Louis	IP	H	R	ER	BB	SO	NP	ERA
Lohse W, 1-0	5⅔	7	1	1	5	2	108	1.59
Rosenthal H, 2	⅓	0	0	0	0	0	6	0.00
Mujica H, 2	⅓	2	0	0	0	0	6	0.00
Boggs H, 2	⅔	0	0	0	0	2	9	0.00
Motte S, 2-2	2	0	0	0	0	0	19	0.00

Inherited runners-scored—Ja.Lopez 2-0, Kontos 1-0, Rosenthal 2-0, Boggs 2-0. **IBB**—off M.Cain (Descalso), off Lohse (Posey). **HBP**—by M.Cain (Jay). **Umpires**—Home, Bill Miller; First, Greg Gibson; Second, Ted Barrett; Third, Jerry Layne; Right, Chris Guccione; Left, Gary Darling. **Time**—3:02 (Rain delay: 3:28). **Attendance**—45,850 (43,975).

NLCS GAME 4

BACK TO THE BRINK

BY HENRY SCHULMAN

Hunter Pence's fiery sermon before Game 3 of the Division Series was organic. It came from the gut and would not have had the same impact had he planned it. He doubts he will repeat it before the Giants begin a new round of Let's See If We Can Survive Tonight.

"It ran its course," Pence said in the quiet aftermath of Thursday night's 8-3 loss to the Cardinals. "There might be a speech. Who knows who's going to say what and what's going to happen? You never know when your backs are against the wall."

At least this is a familiar wall.

After losing Game 4 of the National League Championship Series, with Tim Lincecum's Great Resurrection turning into a great disappointment, the Giants are down three games to one.

For the second time, they need a three-game winning streak to save their season.

For the second time as well, Barry Zito will start a potential elimination game, Game 5 on Friday night, the last of the three at Busch Stadium.

If the Giants win and return the series to San Francisco, Ryan Vogelsong gets Game 6 and Matt Cain Game 7.

The odds are long. Since the LCS became a best-of-seven in 1985, only four of the 33 teams that have fallen behind 3-1 have come back to win.

"The way I look at it," Pence said, "Zito has been tremendous for us. We've got to find a way to get tomorrow. If we get home with Vogelsong and Cain we feel very confident. Everybody should go out and enjoy the game tomorrow. Don't forget

Above: Cardinal first baseman Matt Carpenter celebrates a ground out by the Giants' Pablo Sandoval.
Michael Macor

88 SAN FRANCISCO GIANTS: A RETURN TO THE PINNACLE

how hard we worked to get the right to play in this series."

Pence's roadmap requires a sharp U-turn for a Giants team that has looked inferior to the Cardinals in every way in the two games here, starting with the pitching.

Kyle Lohse was a master of "bend but don't break" in Game 3. Adam Wainwright simply was impenetrable in Game 4. He pounded the strike zone and put Giants hitters on the defensive in so many at-bats.

Both starters carried themselves like winners. Giants starters did the same thing with great results – in the 2010 postseason.

Manager Bruce Bochy shuffled the lineup - he called it a "tweak" – and dropped Pence from fifth to sixth. Hector Sanchez made his first start of the NLCS and batted fifth, while Bochy flip-flopped Buster Posey and Pablo Sandoval in hopes of getting Posey some protection.

It hardly mattered. Posey, Sanchez and Sandoval were 0-for-9 against Wainwright. Sanchez struck out all three times, likely earning him a ticket to watch Zito throw to Posey on Friday.

Pence homered in the second inning for his first RBI of the postseason and the Giants' only run in seven innings against Wainwright. Sandoval hit a meaningless two-run homer in the ninth against Fernando Salas.

"Today and yesterday, they were both very good pitchers," Angel Pagan said. "They kept us off-balance. They were in the zone. Sometimes that happens and you don't have a chance."

Wainwright buried the Giants with his slow curve, which he dropped into the strike zone at will and complemented with a cutter that seemed to start on one corner of the plate and move to the other. Pence said Wainwright "was as good as you're going to see."

Giants hitters had the added pressure of playing from behind all night after Lincecum allowed two first-inning runs.

Seven pitches in, after Jon Jay's single and a four-pitch walk to Matt Carpenter, it was clear the starter Lincecum was not going to channel the bullpen Lincecum, who allowed only four of 28 hitters

Above: Giants starting pitcher Tim Lincecum is taken out after 5 2/3 innings of the National League Championship Series in St. Louis. *Michael Macor*

to reach in 8 1/3 innings.

He let four Cardinals reach in the first inning Thursday.

"For me to go out there was great," Lincecum said, "but I didn't do my job."

There was a clubhouse consensus on the game's key play. It occurred in the fifth inning with the Giants trailing 2-1 and Carpenter on second base after a one-out double.

NATIONAL LEAGUE CHAMPIONSHIP SERIES GAME 4

NLCS GAME 4

Above: The Cardinals' Matt Carpenter is safe at home as the ball got loose from Giants catcher Hector Sanchez in the fifth inning, in Game 4 of the National League Championship. *Michael Macor*

Matt Holliday hit a sinking liner to center that Pagan nearly caught. Carpenter initially had to hold up but was sent home from second anyway. Pagan fired to Brandon Crawford, who threw a one-hopper to Sanchez that beat the runner.

But Sanchez let the ball bounce off his glove. The Cards led 3-1, then 4-1 on an RBI single by Yadier Molina that ended Lincecum's night and perhaps his season.

Jay sealed the win with a two-run double against Jose Mijares in the sixth.

The brightest moment for the Giants was Pence's 451-foot homer a day after he called himself the "goat" of the Giants' Game 3 loss.

SAN FRANCISCO GIANTS: A RETURN TO THE PINNACLE

BOX SCORE

Cardinals 8, Giants 3

Giants	AB	R	H	BI	BB	SO	Avg.
Pagan cf	4	0	2	0	0	0	.333
Scutaro 2b	4	1	2	0	0	0	.471
Posey 1b	4	0	0	0	0	0	.143
Sandoval 3b	4	1	1	2	0	0	.235
H.Sanchez c	4	0	0	0	0	3	.000
Pence rf	4	1	1	1	0	0	.133
G.Blanco lf	3	0	0	0	0	0	.154
B.Crawford ss	2	0	0	0	0	1	.231
Kontos p	0	0	0	0	0	0	—
Mijares p	0	0	0	0	0	0	—
Mota p	0	0	0	0	0	0	—
Affeldt p	0	0	0	0	0	0	—
A.Huff ph	1	0	0	0	0	1	.333
Ja.Lopez p	0	0	0	0	0	0	—
Lincecum p	1	0	0	0	0	1	.000
Arias ss	2	0	0	0	0	0	.000
Totals	**33**	**3**	**6**	**3**	**0**	**6**	

St. Louis	AB	R	H	BI	BB	SO	Avg.
Jay cf	5	1	2	2	0	1	.235
M.Carpenter 1b	3	2	1	0	2	1	.333
Holliday lf	5	1	2	2	0	0	.235
Chambers lf	0	0	0	0	0	0	.000
Craig rf	3	1	1	1	0	1	.083
Y.Molina c	4	1	2	2	0	0	.313
Freese 3b	4	0	1	0	0	1	.267
Descalso 2b	4	1	1	0	0	1	.214
Kozma ss	4	1	2	1	0	1	.286
Wainwright p	1	0	0	0	1	0	.000
S.Robinson ph	1	0	0	0	0	1	.000
Salas p	0	0	0	0	0	0	—
Totals	**34**	**8**	**12**	**8**	**3**	**7**	

Giants	010	000	002	—	3	6	1
St. Louis	200	022	20x	—	8	12	0

E—Sandoval (2). **LOB**—Giants 3, St. Louis 7. **2B**—Scutaro (2), Jay (1), M.Carpenter (1), Y.Molina (1). **3B**—Pagan (1). **HR**—Pence (1), off Wainwright; Sandoval (1), off Salas. **RBIs**—Sandoval 2 (3), Pence (1), Jay 2 (3), Holliday 2 (2), Craig (1), Y.Molina 2 (2), Kozma (2). **CS**—Kozma (1). **S**—Wainwright. **SF**—Craig.

Giants	IP	H	R	ER	BB	SO	NP	ERA
Lincecum L, 0-1	4 2/3	6	4	4	3	3	91	5.40
Kontos	2/3	2	2	2	0	0	17	13.50
Mijares	1/3	1	0	0	0	0	11	0.00
Mota	2/3	2	2	2	0	1	25	27.00
Affeldt	2/3	1	0	0	0	1	11	0.00
Ja.Lopez	1	0	0	0	0	2	13	0.00

St. Louis	IP	H	R	ER	BB	SO	NP	ERA
Wainwright W, 1-0	7	4	1	1	0	5	96	1.29
Salas	2	2	2	2	0	1	28	6.00

Inherited runners-scored—Kontos 1-0, Mijares 2-2, Mota 1-0, Affeldt 1-1. **WP**—Affeldt. **Umpires**—Home, Greg Gibson; First, Ted Barrett; Second, Jerry Layne; Third, Gary Darling; Right, Bill Miller; Left, Chris Guccione. **Time**—3:17. **Attendance**—47,062 (43,975).

The pep-talk champ went deep after getting one himself.

"I talked to him today and he was pretty hard on himself," Bochy said. "I just said, 'We don't do that here.' We all could have done something maybe to help in that ballgame."

On Thursday, the Giants simply looked helpless. That has to change Friday, or else.

NLCS GAME 5

ZITO'S FINEST HOUR

■ BY HENRY SCHULMAN

You have to feel for the people of India, Ecuador, Turkey and points beyond when they dialed up Twitter on Friday and saw the hashtag #RallyZito trending. One could almost hear a worldwide "huh?"

Giants fans got behind Barry Zito in a way they never had before. They changed their Twitter avatars to Zito photos and pushed that tag the way Anheuser-Busch hawks cheap beer in this town.

Zito rewarded the faithful by delivering the National League Championship Series back to San Francisco. He pitched $7^{2}/_{3}$ shutout innings in a 5-0 Game 5 victory, the fourth potential elimination game the Giants have won in this postseason and the 13th consecutive Zito start that ended triumphantly for his team.

Ryan Vogelsong faces Chris Carpenter at AT&T Park in Game 6 on Sunday, a rematch of the Giants' Game 2 win.

Nearly an hour after Sergio Romo closed the win, Zito sat in the interview room and smiled when asked if he knew how furiously Giants fans rallied behind him on Twitter.

"I tried Twitter a couple of years ago. It was a pretty devastating experience for me," Zito said. "I learned not to check the inbox."

He had gotten a huge whiff of the anger from those who felt he fleeced the Giants out of $126 million. After Friday's win, the man who authorized the big check walked into the clubhouse full of glee, but with no I-told-you-sos.

"He's had his ups and downs as a Giant, and he sure rose to the occasion tonight," former managing general partner Peter Magowan said. "We should all be elated at what he did. He's kept us in the season. We've got a shot at the World Series because of what he did tonight.

Above: Giants starting pitcher Barry Zito throws as the Giants take on the Cardinals in Game 5 of the National League Championship Series. *Michael Macor*

Above: Marco Scutaro fields a ball hit into short right field by Shane Robinson in the fifth inning. Robinson was out at first during the National League Championship Series at Busch Stadium in St. Louis, Mo. *Carlos Avila Gonzales*

"He's a good guy. He deserves good things to happen to him."

Good things for the Giants abounded on a frigid night at Busch Stadium.

The Giants took advantage of pitcher Lance Lynn's throwing error to score four unearned runs in the fourth inning. Brandon Crawford's two-out, two-run single was the dagger, Zito's run-scoring bunt single the coup de grace.

Fans on both sides of San Francisco Bay know what four runs of support has meant for Zito: a 126-7 record for his teams.

Pablo Sandoval added a solo homer in the eighth inning against Mitchell Boggs.

The Giants also played inspired defense, with nice plays by Sandoval, Angel Pagan, Hunter Pence and Marco Scutaro, whose fist pump after he dived in the outfield to snag Shane Robinson's fifth-inning grounder was his biggest emotional burst since he arrived.

Sandoval went airborne and lunged to catch an Allen Craig line-drive foul to end the first inning moments after he slammed a foul ball off his right toe so hard that he spent several moments on his hands and knees in agony.

"When you've got a guy like Barry stepping up for you and throwing the ball so well, you've got to do things for him," Sandoval said. "You've got to play hard."

Before the game, Pence said, players were "rallying together" in the clubhouse, "getting focused for the storm to come."

Zito's work made for calmer seas. He did have a short leash, as many folks expected, but not until

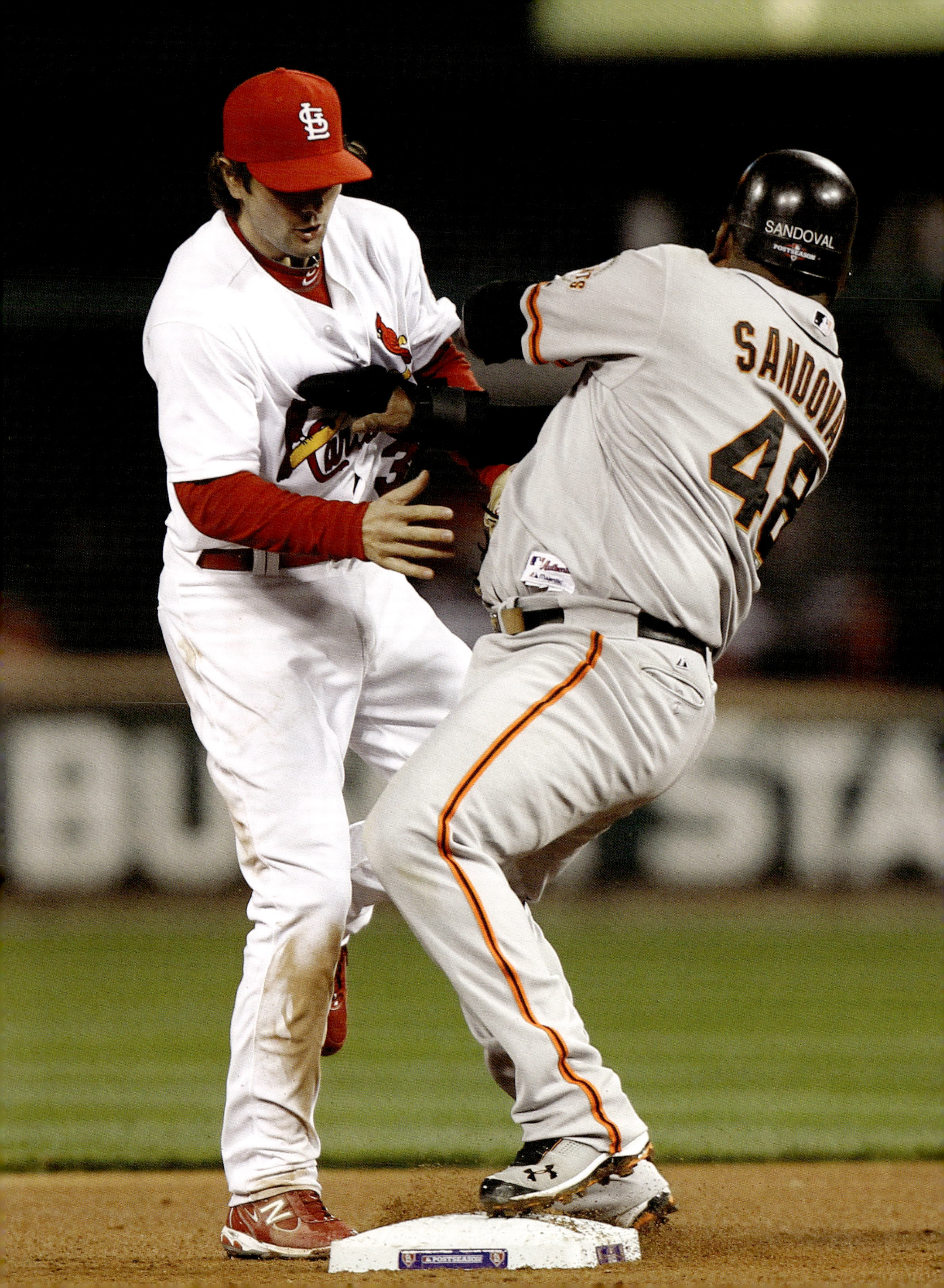
SANDOVAL
48

he became the first Giants starter to reach the eighth inning in their 10 playoff games.

After Carlos Beltran flied out on Zito's season-high 115th pitch, manager Bruce Bochy took him out as a sea of right-handed Cardinals awaited. He had allowed six hits and a walk while striking out seven.

"He was pitching, " St. Louis manager Mike Matheny said. "He was raising eye level. He was in the top of the zone, just above, on the edges. He was moving in and out, back and forth. He was taking speeds off his breaking ball and changeup. That's what pitching is."

The game hinged on two pitches.

With the bases loaded in the second after an intentional walk to Pete Kozma, Zito got Lynn to ground a curveball into a double play that ended the inning.

With one out in the fourth, after singles by Scutaro and Sandoval, Pence hit a chopper to Lynn, who should have gotten one out for sure with an outside shot at a double play. But he bounced a scud off the second-base bag and into center field for an error that got Scutaro home.

Roberto Kelly was back in the first-base coaching box for the first time in the series. When Pence reached the bag, Kelly told him, "There's the break we needed."

With two outs and the bases loaded after Lynn walked Gregor Blanco, Crawford grounded a two-run single over second base to give the Giants a 3-0 lead. Zito then pushed a perfect bunt up the third-base line to score Blanco, the first bunt single of his career.

"I'm known for my Arabian horse gallop, as (Brian) Wilson calls it, " Zito said. "I'm just not that fast."

Great. Now the hashtag #ArabianHorseGallop is going to trend worldwide.

Opposite Page: The Cardinals' Pete Kozma and Giants' Pablo Sandoval get tangled up on a throw to second base after a single by Hunter Pence that scored Marco Scutaro in the fourth inning. *Michael Macor*

BOX SCORE

Giants 5, Cardinals 0

Giants	AB	R	H	BI	BB	SO	Avg.
Pagan cf	5	0	0	0	0	1	.261
Scutaro 2b	4	1	1	0	0	0	.429
Sandoval 3b	4	2	2	1	0	1	.286
Arias 3b	0	0	0	0	0	0	.000
Posey c	4	0	1	0	0	2	.167
Pence rf	4	1	0	0	0	2	.105
Belt 1b	3	0	0	0	1	2	.214
G.Blanco lf	2	1	0	0	2	1	.133
B.Crawford ss	4	0	1	2	0	2	.235
Zito p	2	0	1	1	0	1	.500
S.Casilla p	0	0	0	0	0	0	—
A.Huff ph	1	0	0	0	0	0	.250
Romo p	0	0	0	0	0	0	—
Totals	**33**	**5**	**6**	**4**	**3**	**12**	

St. Louis	AB	R	H	BI	BB	SO	Avg.
Jay cf	4	0	1	0	0	0	.238
Beltran rf	4	0	1	0	0	1	.333
Holliday lf	4	0	0	0	0	3	.190
Craig 1b	4	0	1	0	0	0	.125
Y.Molina c	4	0	2	0	0	0	.350
Freese 3b	4	0	1	0	0	1	.263
Descalso 2b	4	0	1	0	0	1	.222
Kozma ss	2	0	0	0	1	1	.250
Lynn p	1	0	0	0	0	0	.000
J.Kelly p	0	0	0	0	0	0	—
S.Robinson ph	1	0	0	0	0	0	.000
Rosenthal p	0	0	0	0	0	0	—
Boggs p	0	0	0	0	0	0	—
Schumaker ph	1	0	0	0	0	1	.000
Mujica p	0	0	0	0	0	0	—
Totals	**33**	**0**	**7**	**0**	**1**	**8**	

Giants	000	400	010	—	5	6	0
St. Louis	000	000	000	—	0	7	1

E—Lynn (1). **LOB**—Giants 5, St. Louis 7. **2B**—Craig (1), Freese (2). **HR**—Sandoval (2), off Boggs. **RBIs**—Sandoval (4), B.Crawford 2 (4), Zito (1). **SB**—Belt (1), Beltran (1). **S**—Zito. **Runners moved up**—Y.Molina. **GIDP**—Lynn. **DP**—Giants 1 (B.Crawford, Scutaro, Belt).

Giants	IP	H	R	ER	BB	SO	NP	ERA
Zito W, 1-0	7 2/3	6	0	0	1	6	115	0.00
S.Casilla	1/3	0	0	0	0	1	7	0.00
Romo	1	1	0	0	0	1	21	0.00

St. Louis	IP	H	R	ER	BB	SO	NP	ERA
Lynn L, 0-1	3 2/3	4	4	0	2	6	66	4.91
J.Kelly	1 1/3	1	0	0	0	1	12	0.00
Rosenthal	2	0	0	0	0	4	27	0.00
Boggs	1	1	1	1	1	1	24	3.38
Mujica	1	0	0	0	0	0	7	0.00

Inherited runners-scored—S.Casilla 1-0, J.Kelly 2-0. **IBB**—off Zito (Kozma). **Umpires**—Home, Ted Barrett; First, Jerry Layne; Second, Gary Darling; Third, Chris Guccione; Right, Greg Gibson; Left, Bill Miller. **Time**—3:03. **Attendance**—47,075 (43,975).

NLCS GAME 6

NEVER SAY DIE

■ BY HENRY SCHULMAN

Nobody has a better perspective on the two unsinkable teams that will play for the National League pennant Monday night. Ryan Theriot wore the birds on the bat when the Cardinals roared back from the brink twice to win the 2011 World Series. Now he wears black and orange and has seen the Giants win five elimination games.

"You're seeing so much of the character of both of these ballclubs," Theriot said after the Giants dominated St. Louis in Sunday's 6-1 win.

"When you've been around this game a long time, you know it takes more than sheer talent. You've really, truly got to trust the guy next to you. This team has it. That team over there has it, and now it comes down to two great pitchers who've had great years. We're going to have a lot of fun."

Matt Cain faces Kyle Lohse in a rematch of the Cardinals' Game 3 win. It will be the first Game 7 played in San Francisco since the 1962 World Series.

If Cain can ride the wave of zeroes thrown up by Barry Zito in Game 5 and Ryan Vogelsong in Game 6, the Giants will have an excellent shot at becoming the second team in major-league history to win six elimination games in a single postseason.

The 1985 Royals rebounded from 3-1 deficits to win the American League Championship Series against the Blue Jays and the World Series against the Cardinals.

Sunday's game was no contest because the Giants followed a charged first inning from Vogelsong to take a 1-0 lead, then pounced on Chris Carpenter

Above: Giants relief pitcher Sergio Romo celebrates the final out of the Giants' 6-1 win over the St. Louis Cardinals. *Lance Iversen*

Above: St. Louis Cardinals shortstop Pete Kozma misplays Giants pitcher Ryan Vogelsong's RBI base hit in the second inning of Game 6 of the NLCS at AT&T Park. *Lance Iversen*

like a cat on tuna fish with a four-run second.

A resurgent Pablo Sandoval was a keystone. He doubled to set up Buster Posey's scoring groundball in the first inning, then singled home the Giants' fifth run, in the second, after Marco Scutaro continued to punish the Cardinals with a two-run double.

Vogelsong allowed one run on four hits in seven innings, just as he did in Game 2, with one big difference. In the earlier game, he struck out four. On Sunday he struck out a career-high nine.

In three postseason starts, Vogelsong has pitched 19 innings and allowed three runs, one per game. "He was unbelievable," center fielder Angel Pagan said. "After the catcher, I have the best view. All of his pitches were sharp. He kept everything down.

The best part was we put runs on the board early. That was the difference. He had the confidence to keep going after the hitters."

Vogelsong confirmed that.

"I pitch like it's 0-0, 1-0 all the time, " he said. "But to have a cushion like that early definitely allows you to attack the plate a little bit more, especially with the offense they have over there. They swing the bats well and they strike quick, and it's usually multiple runs."

The St. Louis sixth-inning run ended a 15-inning drought. Carlos Beltran doubled and Allen Craig singled.

Buster Posey called Vogelsong's stuff "electric," which Jon Jay learned when Vogelsong blew a

NATIONAL LEAGUE CHAMPIONSHIP SERIES GAME 6

NLCS GAME 6

Above: The Giants' Brandon Belt shatters his bat in the eighth innning but still singled in Game 6 of the National League Championship Series at AT&T Park. *Michael Macor*

98　SAN FRANCISCO GIANTS: A RETURN TO THE PINNACLE

94-mph fastball past him for strike three to start the game.

Vogelsong threw 13 consecutive fastballs before pulling a 1-2 changeup out of his quiver to strike out Beltran. Vogelsong ended the first with a 93-mph two-seamer to Craig that started off the plate and zipped over the corner.

The Giant then scored when Posey hit a grounder to third baseman David Freese's backhand. Freese had a great shot to nail Scutaro at home until the ball momentarily rolled around his glove. Freese had to go to first for the out.

A slumping Brandon Belt launched the four-run second with a triple into the vast right-center acreage. Beltran tried to deke him by lifting his glove, but Belt wasn't buying what his former teammate was selling.

"He's done it to me before, and he's gotten me out at second before," Belt said. "I wasn't going to fall for it again. As soon as I hit the ball I said to myself, 'Run as quick as you can until he catches it or throws it back in.'"

Gregor Blanco struck out before Carpenter walked Brandon Crawford intentionally to face Vogelsong.

In a similar situation in Game 3, manager Bruce Bochy had Cain sacrifice. But the Giants were behind then. This time, they had a lead, which allowed Bochy to send Crawford and let Vogelsong pull the bat back and swing away.

He hit a grounder to shortstop Pete Kozma, who booted the ball for that big error the Giants seem to get in every postseason win. Belt would have scored either way, but Vogelsong was safe at first.

After Pagan struck out, Scutaro roped a double into the left-field corner to score Crawford and Vogelsong for a 4-0 lead – a huge advantage that Vogelsong could not appreciate immediately.

"I was looking for the oxygen first, running from first base," Vogelsong joked before saying how much the lead helped him.

"Sorry, brother," Scutaro said, thrilled that he made Vogelsong take that 270-foot dash.

"We're 27 outs from the World Series," he said. "For me that's priceless."

BOX SCORE

Giants 6, Cardinals 1

St. Louis	AB	R	H	BI	BB	SO	Avg.
Jay cf	4	0	0	0	0	1	.200
M.Carpenter 1b	3	0	1	0	1	0	.333
Beltran rf	4	1	1	0	0	2	.313
Craig lf	4	0	1	1	0	2	.150
Y.Molina c	4	0	0	0	0	0	.292
Freese 3b	4	0	0	0	0	3	.217
Descalso 2b	4	0	0	0	0	2	.227
Kozma ss	3	0	1	0	0	0	.263
C.Carpenter p	1	0	0	0	0	1	.500
Schumaker ph	1	0	0	0	0	0	.000
S.Miller p	0	0	0	0	0	0	—
S.Robinson ph	1	0	0	0	0	0	.000
Salas p	0	0	0	0	0	0	—
Rzepczynski p	0	0	0	0	0	0	—
Mujica p	0	0	0	0	0	0	—
Totals	**33**	**1**	**5**	**1**	**1**	**11**	

Giants	AB	R	H	BI	BB	SO	Avg.
Pagan cf	5	0	0	0	0	1	.214
Scutaro 2b	3	2	2	2	1	0	.458
Sandoval 3b	4	0	2	1	0	0	.320
Arias 3b	0	0	0	0	0	0	.000
Posey c	4	0	0	1	0	1	.136
Pence rf	4	0	1	0	0	3	.130
Belt 1b	4	2	2	0	0	1	.278
G.Blanco lf	4	0	1	0	0	2	.158
B.Crawford ss	2	1	0	0	2	2	.211
Vogelsong p	3	1	0	1	0	1	.200
Affeldt p	0	0	0	0	0	0	—
S.Casilla p	0	0	0	0	0	0	—
Theriot ph	1	0	1	1	0	0	.667
Romo p	0	0	0	0	0	0	—
Totals	**34**	**6**	**9**	**6**	**3**	**11**	

St.Louis	000	001	000	—	1	5	1
Giants	140	000	01x	—	6	9	1

E—Kozma (1), G.Blanco (1). **LOB**—St. Louis 6, Giants 7. **2B**—Beltran (3), Scutaro (3), Sandoval (1), G.Blanco (1). **3B**—Belt (1). **RBIs**—Craig (2), Scutaro 2 (4), Sandoval (5), Posey (1), Vogelsong (1), Theriot (3).

St. Louis	IP	H	R	ER	BB	SO	NP	ERA
C.Carpenter L, 0-2	4	6	5	2	2	6	76	4.50
S.Miller	2	1	0	0	0	2	37	5.40
Salas	1 1/3	0	0	0	0	2	15	4.15
Rzepczynski	1/3	1	1	1	1	1	13	6.75
Mujica	1/3	1	0	0	0	0	3	0.00

Giants	IP	H	R	ER	BB	SO	NP	ERA
Vogelsong W, 2-0	7	4	1	1	1	9	102	1.29
Affeldt	2/3	1	0	0	0	1	10	0.00
S.Casilla	1/3	0	0	0	0	0	3	0.00
Romo	1	0	0	0	0	1	8	0.00

Inherited runners-scored—Mujica 2-1, S.Casilla 1-0. **IBB**—off C.Carpenter (B.Crawford). **Umpires**—Home, Jerry Layne; First, Gary Darling; Second, Chris Guccione; Third, Bill Miller; Right, Ted Barrett; Left, Greg Gibson. **Time**—2:55. **Attendance**—43,070 (41,915).

NLCS GAME 7

ALL THE WAY BACK!
SERIES MVP SCUTARO GETS 3 MORE HITS IN BLOWOUT

■ BY HENRY SCHULMAN

As rain pounded the field in the ninth inning, second baseman Marco Scutaro spread his arms and looked to the heavens. As the water soaked his face, he beamed a 100,000-watt smile.

Moments later, he looked up again. This time his ticket to the World Series, a Matt Holliday popup, was falling his way. As Sergio Romo bounced on the mound like a kid on a pogo stick, Scutaro squeezed his glove and the Giants had a most improbable pennant.

Down three games to one in the National League Championship Series, they dominated the Cardinals over the final three games and bulldozed the defending World Series champions 9-0 Monday night.

The Giants outscored St. Louis 20-1 in Games 5, 6, and 7 and won a decisive seventh game for the first time in franchise history, while joining the 1996 Braves and 2003 Marlins as the only teams to overcome a 3-1 deficit to win an NLCS.

"How fitting that it happened in the rain," team president Larry Baer said. "October is our most beautiful month in San Francisco and it's pouring outside. It's crazy, just like everything this team has done."

Now the Giants will play the well-rested Detroit Tigers in a World Series that seemed out of reach so many times. Manager Bruce Bochy's boys won six elimination wins to get there, the second time a team has eluded the reaper's scythe that many times in a single postseason.

In doing so they ended the season of another team that had a unique way of slipping from mortality's reach. The Giants formally ended the Cardinals' reign as World Series champions.

Above: Angel Pagan kisses one of his daughters after the Giants' victory. *Pete Kiehart*

100 SAN FRANCISCO GIANTS: A RETURN TO THE PINNACLE

Above: Giants' Angel Pagan reaches for home plate as he scores against the Cardinals in Game 7 of the NLCS at AT&T Park. *Lance Iversen*

The Giants also gave the faithful a thrill it could not enjoy in 2010, a postseason series-clinching at AT&T Park. Many will return for Game 1 of the Series on Wednesday night.

Romo was asked to get the final out of a Game 7 blowout as rain fell so hard the area behind third base could have been called Lake Panda. Home-plate umpire Gary Darling momentarily stopped play so the grounds crew could apply dry dirt to the infield.

That only heightened the anticipation for 43,056 fans who did not seem to care a whit about getting drenched. They did not pop open umbrellas. They just waved their orange towels.

When play resumed, Romo got Holliday – of course – to pop up to Scutaro – of course. The entire narrative of their collision in Game 2 came full circle as the Giants reached their second World Series in three seasons.

"I was just like praying, 'Please, I've got to catch this ball,' " Scutaro said. "I got kind of lucky, too. When he hit the flyball the rain stopped a little bit. A couple of minutes earlier maybe I don't catch it."

Romo stood in his corner of another clubhouse party and had to laugh.

"I'm from the desert, so I don't know much about rain," he said. "I was very happy to go out there in the rain, the sunshine, it doesn't matter. I just wanted to play with these guys and make them smile, and now we're going to the World Series."

The mob of newly minted National League champs navigated toward Scutaro after the catch, which also was fitting. The midseason acquisition won the series Most Valuable Player award in a runaway.

He batted .500 and tied a League Championship

NATIONAL LEAGUE CHAMPIONSHIP SERIES GAME 7   101

NLCS GAME 7

Above: Giants pitcher Matt Cain throws in the first inning during Game 7 of the NLCS in San Francisco. *Lance Iversen*

Series record with 14 hits, two of which contributed to a burst of seven Giants runs in the first three innings that turned what was supposed to be a tense, winner-take-all game into a 3-hour, 35-minute victory lap.

Scutaro also broke Will Clark's franchise record of 13 hits in a single postseason series, which he set in the 1989 NLCS.

But Scutaro did not have the Game 7 hit that will become etched in Giants postseason lore.

They were leading 2-0 in the third inning, one run scoring on a single by winning pitcher Matt Cain, when they loaded the bases with nobody out to chase starter Kyle Lohse. The rally started with a Scutaro single, which Pablo Sandoval followed with a double.

Joe Kelly relieved Lohse and threw one pitch to Hunter Pence, who was 3-for-24 in the series. The ball broke Pence's bat as he made contact. Replays showed that as the barrel busted, the bat hit the ball two more times, imparting wicked spin and forcing the ball to change course.

That explains why shortstop Pete Kozma initially broke to his right, then had to do a 180 and go left. His diving attempt was futile. The ball rolled into center field and two runs scored on the hit. Buster Posey then rumbled home from first for a 5-0 lead when Jon Jay bobbled the ball.

Pence said he did not feel the bat hit the ball more than once, but he saw it on the replay. So did Clark, a Giants special instructor.

"I've never hit a ball like that. I've never seen a ball hit like that," Clark said. "That's the beauty of baseball.

"We've talked about the baseball gods before. The baseball gods were shining on the Giants."

Above: Sergio Romo celebrates after the final out of the game as Buster Posey approaches him.
Carlos Avila Gonzalez

BOX SCORE

Giants 9, Cardinals 0

St. Louis	AB	R	H	BI	BB	SO	Avg.
Jay cf	4	0	1	0	1	2	.207
Beltran rf	4	0	1	0	1	0	.300
Holliday lf	4	0	1	0	0	0	.200
Craig 1b	4	0	0	0	0	0	.125
Y.Molina c	4	0	4	0	0	0	.393
Freese 3b	3	0	0	0	1	1	.192
Descalso 2b	3	0	0	0	0	1	.200
T.Cruz ph	1	0	0	0	0	1	.000
Motte p	0	0	0	0	0	0	—
Kozma ss	3	0	0	0	1	2	.227
Lohse p	1	0	0	0	0	0	.000
J.Kelly p	0	0	0	0	0	0	—
Mujica p	0	0	0	0	0	0	—
Chambers ph	1	0	0	0	0	0	.000
Rosenthal p	0	0	0	0	0	0	—
S.Robinson ph	1	0	0	0	0	1	.000
Boggs p	0	0	0	0	0	0	—
Salas p	0	0	0	0	0	0	—
Schumaker 2b	1	0	0	0	0	0	.000
Totals	**34**	**0**	**7**	**0**	**4**	**8**	

Giants	AB	R	H	BI	BB	SO	Avg.
Pagan cf	5	1	2	1	0	1	.242
Scutaro 2b	4	1	3	0	1	0	.500
Sandoval 3b	4	1	1	1	1	0	.310
S.Casilla p	0	0	0	0	0	0	—
Ja.Lopez p	0	0	0	0	0	0	—
Romo p	0	0	0	0	0	0	—
Posey c	4	1	1	0	1	0	.154
Pence rf	5	1	2	2	0	2	.179
Belt 1b	5	2	2	1	0	0	.304
G.Blanco lf	3	2	1	0	2	0	.182
B.Crawford ss	4	0	1	1	0	1	.217
M.Cain p	3	0	1	1	0	2	.400
Affeldt p	0	0	0	0	0	0	—
A.Huff ph	1	0	0	0	0	0	.200
Arias 3b	0	0	0	0	0	0	.000
Totals	**38**	**9**	**14**	**7**	**5**	**6**	

St.Louis	000	000	000	—	0	7	2
Giants	115	000	11x	—	9	14	0

E—Jay (1), Kozma (2). **LOB**—St. Louis 12, Giants 10. **2B**—Sandoval (2), Pence (1). **HR**—Belt (1), off Motte. **RBIs**—Pagan (2), Sandoval (6), Pence 2 (3), Belt (2), B.Crawford (5), M.Cain (1). **SB**—Beltran (2), Descalso (1). **Runners moved up**—Beltran, Holliday, Sandoval, B.Crawford. **GIDP**—A.Huff. **DP**—St. Louis 1 (Descalso, Kozma, Craig).

St. Louis	IP	H	R	ER	BB	SO	NP	ERA
Lohse L, 1-1	2	6	5	5	1	1	46	7.04
J.Kelly	2/3	2	2	2	2	1	26	4.50
Mujica	1 1/3	1	0	0	0	0	14	0.00
Rosenthal	2	1	0	0	1	4	34	0.00
Boggs	2/3	3	1	1	1	0	22	5.40
Salas	1/3	0	0	0	0	0	3	3.86
Motte	1	1	1	1	0	0	14	2.25

Giants	IP	H	R	ER	BB	SO	NP	ERA
M.Cain W, 1-1	5 2/3	5	0	0	1	4	102	2.19
Affeldt	1 1/3	0	0	0	1	2	18	0.00
S.Casilla	2/3	2	0	0	0	0	17	0.00
Ja.Lopez	1	0	0	0	2	2	25	0.00
Romo	1/3	0	0	0	0	0	4	0.00

Lohse pitched to 3 batters in the 3rd. **Inherited runners-scored**—J.Kelly 3-3, Mujica 3-0, Salas 2-0, Affeldt 2-0, Ja.Lopez 2-0, Romo 2-0. **HBP**—by M.Cain (Holliday). **WP**—S.Casilla, Romo. **Umpires**—Home, Gary Darling; First, Chris Guccione; Second, Bill Miller; Third, Greg Gibson; Right, Jerry Layne; Left, Ted Barrett. **Time**—3:35. **Attendance**—43,056 (41,915).

WORLD SERIES GAME 1

PANDAMONIUM

BY HENRY SCHULMAN

Buster Posey was on deck, the best spot in the house to watch Pablo Sandoval engrave his name alongside Babe Ruth's in the World Series record book. Posey greeted Sandoval at home plate after each of the Panda's three home runs, curious to see the look on his face.

"He was fired up after the first one," Posey said. "He was fired up after the second one. After the third one he was taken aback a little bit. I think he was trying to soak in the moment."

It was a moment that Sandoval will not forget. Nor will the 42,855 fans who attended the Giants'

Above: Giants' third baseman Pablo Sandoval returns to the dugout in the fifth inning after hitting his third homer of the night. *Michael Macor*

104 SAN FRANCISCO GIANTS: A RETURN TO THE PINNACLE

Above: Tigers' pitcher Justin Verlander throws in the first inning during Game 1 of the World Series in San Francisco. *Lance Iversen*

8-3 Series-opening victory Wednesday night and saw Sandoval join Ruth, Reggie Jackson and Albert Pujols as the only players to hit three home runs in a World Series game. Ruth did it twice.

Sandoval homered in his first three plate appearances, twice off Justin Verlander, whom the Giants swatted for five runs in four innings. Sandoval then broke his bat on the third home run, in the fifth inning against reliever Al Alburquerque, to cement his spot in World Series lore.

Sandoval batted again in the seventh and hit a mere single against deposed Tigers closer Jose Valverde. His 13 total bases rank second all-time in the World Series behind the 14 that Pujols collected in his three-homer game against Texas last year.

Later, Sandoval confirmed Posey's suspicion that the final home run felt different.

"I was stepping on second base and thinking, 'Wow'" Sandoval said. "I can't believe I hit three home runs in a game. When you feel great, everything goes your way."

The 26-year-old third baseman became the first

WORLD SERIES GAME 1

Above: The Giants Barry Zito pitches in the first inning of Game 1 of the World Series in San Francisco. *Michael Macor*

Giant to homer in the first inning of a World Series game since Mel Ott in 1933 when he turned on a 95-mph, neck-high fastball and sent it into the bleachers in right-center.

Batting coach Hensley Meulens said he liked the way Sandoval attacked that pitch in the "zone." Asked whose zone rises to chin level, Meulens smiled and said, "Only his."

Sandoval's second homer came in the third inning after the Giants added a run on a two-out Marco Scutaro single. The rally began when Angel Pagan hit a groundball off third base that scooted into left field for a double, yet another nutty break for the Giants in a postseason that keeps rolling their way.

When Sandoval got the count to 2-0, pitching coach Jeff Jones visited the mound. Before Jones was back in his seat, Verlander threw a 95-mph fastball and Sandoval blasted it the other way, over the left-field fence, for his second homer and a 4-0 lead. Verlander had a one-word reaction on the mound.

Above: Giants third baseman Pablo Sandoval gestures while rounding the bases after hitting his second home run of the game in the third inning. *Michael Macor*

WORLD SERIES: GAME 1   107

WORLD SERIES GAME 1

Giants left fielder Gregor Blanco makes a diving catch in the sixth inning at AT&T Park. *Beck Diefenbach*

Giants left fielder Gregor Blanco makes the play on a line drive hit by Tigers third baseman Miguel Cabrera in the third inning of Game 1 of the World Series. *Beck Diefenbach*

108 SAN FRANCISCO GIANTS: A RETURN TO THE PINNACLE

"Wow."

Sandoval hit an Alburquerque slider to center for his third home run, making him the first Giant to hit three in one game at AT&T Park. The only other player to do it was the Dodgers' Kevin Elster in the stadium's first regular-season game in 2000.

Counting his three-run triple in their first meeting, at the All-Star Game, Sandoval is 3-for-3 with 11 total bases and six RBIs against Verlander, the 2011 American League MVP. For the stat-minded fan, that's a slash line of 1.000/1.000/3.667.

Aubrey Huff, the last Giant to hit three homers in a game, marveled at the feat.

"It's hard enough to do a three-homer game in regular season much less in a World Series game against a pitcher in his prime on top of his game like Verlander," Huff said. "That's the most amazing thing. It's not like he's hitting them off some guy throwing 86."

Almost masked by Sandoval's feat was another shutdown effort from the now-venerated Barry Zito (one run in 5 2/3 innings), more dominating relief from Tim Lincecum, who retired his seven hitters and struck out five, and the Giants' ability to go off script and KO Verlander in four innings after he blew through the A's twice and the Yankees once before he got to San Francisco.

His final insult Wednesday was an RBI single by Zito in the fourth.

"This offense is just confident," reliever Jeremy Affeldt said. "When offenses get hot, sometimes it doesn't matter who's pitching."

So is the defense, which played a big role again. Gregor Blanco made two diving catches in left field with runners on to support Zito, who pitched the Giants to their first Game 1 win this October. The team's win streak behind Zito reached 14 games.

Madison Bumgarner faces Doug Fister in Game 2 on Thursday night. Fister probably went to bed Wednesday thinking about how to attack Sandoval.

"Panda's a guy we want on that kind of a roll," Lincecum said. "Panda's the kind of guy who will take that into tomorrow."

BOX SCORE

Giants 8, Tigers 3

Detroit	AB	R	H	BI	BB	SO	Avg.
A.Jackson cf	4	1	2	0	0	1	.500
Infante 2b	4	0	1	0	0	1	.250
Mi.Cabrera 3b	3	0	1	1	1	1	.333
Fielder 1b	4	0	1	0	0	0	.250
D.Young lf	4	1	2	0	0	0	.500
Jh.Peralta ss	4	1	1	2	0	2	.250
A.Garcia rf	3	0	0	0	0	1	.000
Dirks ph	1	0	0	0	0	0	.000
Avila c	3	0	0	0	1	1	.000
Verlander p	1	0	0	0	0	0	.000
Worth ph	1	0	0	0	0	1	.000
Alburquerque p	0	0	0	0	0	0	—
Berry ph	1	0	0	0	0	0	.000
Valverde p	0	0	0	0	0	0	—
Benoit p	0	0	0	0	0	0	—
Porcello p	0	0	0	0	0	0	—
R.Santiago ph	1	0	0	0	0	0	.000
Totals	34	3	8	3	2	8	

Giants	AB	R	H	BI	BB	SO	Avg.
Pagan cf	4	2	2	0	0	0	.500
Scutaro 2b	4	2	2	2	0	0	.500
Sandoval 3b	4	3	4	4	0	0	1.000
Arias 3b	0	0	0	0	0	0	—
Posey c	4	0	2	1	0	1	.500
Pence rf	4	0	0	0	0	3	.000
Belt 1b	3	1	0	0	1	1	.000
G.Blanco lf	4	0	0	0	0	3	.000
B.Crawford ss	4	0	0	0	0	0	.000
Zito p	2	0	1	1	0	1	.500
Lincecum p	1	0	0	0	0	1	.000
A.Huff ph	1	0	0	0	0	0	.000
Mijares p	0	0	0	0	0	0	—
Kontos p	0	0	0	0	0	0	—
Affeldt p	0	0	0	0	0	0	—
Totals	35	8	11	8	1	10	

Detroit	000 001 002 —	3	8	0
Giants	103 110 20x —	8	11	0

LOB—Detroit 6, Giants 4. **2B**—A.Jackson (1), Pagan 2 (2). **HR**—Jh.Peralta (1), off Kontos; Sandoval 2 (2), off Verlander 2; Sandoval (3), off Alburquerque. **RBIs**—Mi.Cabrera (1), Jh.Peralta 2 (2), Scutaro 2 (2), Sandoval 4 (4), Posey (1), Zito (1). **Runners moved up**—Infante, B.Crawford. **GIDP**—D.Young. **DP**—Giants 1 (Posey, Scutaro).

Detroit	IP	H	R	ER	BB	SO	NP	ERA
Verlander L, 0-1	4	6	5	5	1	4	98	11.25
Alburquerque	2	1	1	1	0	2	28	4.50
Valverde	1/3	4	2	2	0	1	18	54.00
Benoit	2/3	0	0	0	0	2	10	0.00
Porcello	1	0	0	0	0	1	7	0.00

Giants	IP	H	R	ER	BB	SO	NP	ERA
Zito W, 1-0	5 2/3	6	1	1	1	3	81	1.59
Lincecum	2 1/3	0	0	0	0	5	32	0.00
Mijares	1/3	0	0	0	0	0	3	0.00
Kontos	1/3	2	2	2	1	0	17	54.00
Affeldt	1/3	0	0	0	0	0	1	0.00

Inherited runners-scored—Benoit 2-0, Lincecum 2-0, Affeldt 1-0. **WP**—Benoit. **Umpires**—Home, Gerry Davis; First, Dan Iassogna; Second, Fieldin Culbreth; Third, Brian O'Nora; Right, Joe West; Left, Brian Gorman. **Time**—3:26. **Attendance**—42,855 (41,915).

WORLD SERIES GAME 2

HALFWAY THERE

BY HENRY SCHULMAN

The Giants can hire every leprechaun in the Irish Yellow Pages, conjure every spirit who owes them a favor from a past life and get all the nutty, goofy bounces they are enjoying this October.

But they would not be sitting pretty in the 2012 World Series without something more tangible. Their starting pitchers, the core of this team, have become the impenetrable fortress they are expected to be.

A refreshed and mechanically recalibrated Madison Bumgarner joined the ticket Thursday night and fired seven two-hit innings in a 2-0 victory against the Tigers that landed the Giants in an unfamiliar spot – in control of a postseason series.

"All of the starters in the rotation are doing a great job," left fielder Gregor Blanco said. "He's the only one who still needed to do it, and he did. I know he's happy about it."

The rest of the team has to be ecstatic that the starting four dragged the Giants from the brink of elimination into the World Series with wins over the Cardinals in the last three games of the National League Championship Series, then continued their roll to leave the Giants in a historically favorable position.

Each of the past eight teams to take a lead of two games to none in the World Series, and 14 of the past 15, went on to celebrate a championship. That includes the 2010 Giants.

In a winning streak that reached five games, the Giants have outscored the Cardinals and Tigers 30-4,

Above: Giants pitcher Madison Bumgarner reacts after retiring the side in the sixth inning. *Lance Iversen*

110 SAN FRANCISCO GIANTS: A RETURN TO THE PINNACLE

Above: The Giants celebrate their victory. Left to right: Gregor Blanco, Brandon Crawford, Hunter Pence, and Angel Pagan in the air. The Giants defeated the Tigers in Game 2 of the World Series 2-0 at AT&T Park. *Brant Ward*

which surprises Ryan Vogelsong – to a point.

"It's happening at a great time that we're all throwing the ball well at the same time, but it's not something we haven't seen from ourselves this year," Vogelsong said. "Now it's up to me and Cain to go to Detroit and keep it going."

Vogelsong faces Anibal Sanchez in Game 3 at Comerica Park on Saturday, with Matt Cain facing Max Scherzer on Sunday. Game 5 on Monday would feature Barry Zito vs. Justin Verlander II. If the Series returns to San Francisco for Game 6, you can bet Bumgarner will get the start.

The 23-year-old left-hander was energized by a 10-day break and sharp after adjusting his delivery to reduce his backward rotation.

He allowed a Delmon Young double in the second, an Omar Infante infield hit in the sixth, two walks and a hit batter. He also struck out eight.

WORLD SERIES: GAME 2

WORLD SERIES GAME 2

Above: Giants left fielder Gregor Blanco bunts in the seventh inning during Game 2 of the World Series. *Lance Iversen*

Above: Angel Pagan steals second base as Omar Infante awaits the throw. Pagan eventually scored the second run.
Brant Ward

His sense of humor was sharp, too.

Asked if he sensed a difference between this game and his poor efforts earlier in the postseason, Bumgarner said, "Yeah, I went into the seventh inning instead of getting taken out in the third."

Detroit's Doug Fister was almost as good, even after taking a Blanco line drive off his head in the second inning.

The teams were locked in a scoreless duel until Hunter Pence chased Fister with a leadoff single in the seventh. Lefty reliever Drew Smyly made a critical mistake by walking his first hitter, Brandon Belt.

Blanco then provided the night's "you're kidding me" moment for the Giants when he rolled a bunt up the third-base line. Base coach Tim Flannery was so sure it would roll foul that he was hoping the Tigers would pick it up. But they let it roll, and it

WORLD SERIES: GAME 2

WORLD SERIES GAME 2

Above: Tigers first baseman Prince Fielder argues with home plate umpire Dan Iassogna as he's called out in the second inning during Game 2 of the World Series at AT&T Park. *Michael Macor*

114 SAN FRANCISCO GIANTS: A RETURN TO THE PINNACLE

stopped inside the chalk.

Home-plate umpire Dan Iassogna stood over the ball for several seconds before shooting his arm toward fair territory.

The bases were loaded with no outs, and Flannery just had to shake his head at another crazy happening for his team.

"You just go home and thank the higher power of whoever's in charge, and you try not to piss the other ones off," Flannery said.

The Giants took a 1-0 lead when the Tigers played the infield back and Brandon Crawford grounded into a double play. The Giants added insurance in the eighth when Angel Pagan scored on Pence's sacrifice fly.

The game turned earlier on another excellent Giants defensive play.

After Bumgarner hit Prince Fielder to start the second, Young smashed his double past third base. The ball hit the wall past the Giants' bullpen and ricocheted away from Blanco, who retrieved it quickly as third-base coach Gene Lamont inexplicably sent the lumbering Fielder home with nobody out.

Blanco overthrew Crawford, but Marco Scutaro was behind the cutoff man. He caught the ball and relayed it home to Buster Posey. Posey sanely stood out of Fielder's way and applied a swipe tag on Fielder's backside before the big Tiger's front leg brushed the plate.

Detroit did not get another runner to second base.

Santiago Casilla and Sergio Romo each retired their three hitters to send the crowd of 42,982 home thinking a second championship in three years is in the bag.

The Giants do not feel that way, of course, but they are thrilled to be ahead for a change.

"Oh, my God. It feels pretty good," Blanco said. "I came to the park today with my mind that today's game was going to be the biggest of the Series. If we win this game, they're going to be under pressure now."

BOX SCORE

Giants 2, Tigers 0

Detroit	AB	R	H	BI	BB	SO	Avg.
A.Jackson cf	3	0	0	0	1	3	.286
Infante 2b	4	0	1	0	0	2	.250
Mi.Cabrera 3b	2	0	0	0	1	0	.200
Fielder 1b	2	0	0	0	0	0	.167
D.Young lf	3	0	1	0	0	1	.429
D.Kelly lf-rf	0	0	0	0	0	0	—
Jh.Peralta ss	3	0	0	0	0	0	.143
A.Garcia rf	2	0	0	0	0	1	.000
Dirks ph-rf	1	0	0	0	0	0	.000
Dotel p	0	0	0	0	0	0	—
Coke p	0	0	0	0	0	0	—
G.Laird c	3	0	0	0	0	1	.000
Fister p	2	0	0	0	0	1	.000
Smyly p	0	0	0	0	0	0	—
Berry lf	1	0	0	0	0	0	.000
Totals	26	0	2	0	2	9	

Giants	AB	R	H	BI	BB	SO	Avg.
Pagan cf	3	1	0	0	1	1	.286
Scutaro 2b	4	0	0	0	0	1	.250
Sandoval 3b	3	0	1	0	1	0	.714
Romo p	0	0	0	0	0	0	—
Posey c	3	0	1	0	1	0	.429
Pence rf	3	1	1	1	0	0	.143
Belt 1b	3	0	0	0	1	2	.000
G.Blanco lf	3	0	2	0	0	0	.286
B.Crawford ss	2	0	0	0	1	0	.000
Bumgarner p	2	0	0	0	0	1	.000
Theriot ph	1	0	0	0	0	1	.000
S.Casilla p	0	0	0	0	0	0	—
Arias 3b	0	0	0	0	0	0	—
Totals	27	2	5	1	5	6	

Detroit	000	000	000	—	0	2	0
Giants	000	000	11x	—	2	5	0

LOB—Detroit 2, Giants 7. **2B**—D.Young (1). **RBIs**—Pence (1). **SB**—Pagan (1). **CS**—Infante (1). **SF**—Pence. **GIDP**—Fielder, B.Crawford. **DP**—Detroit 1 (Infante, Jh.Peralta, Fielder); Giants 1 (Bumgarner, B.Crawford, Belt).

Detroit	IP	H	R	ER	BB	SO	NP	ERA
Fister L, 0-1	6	4	1	1	1	3	114	1.50
Smyly	1 1/3	1	1	1	3	2	33	6.75
Dotel	1/3	0	0	0	1	0	10	0.00
Coke	1/3	0	0	0	0	1	6	0.00

Giants	IP	H	R	ER	BB	SO	NP	ERA
Bumgarner W, 1-0	7	2	0	0	2	8	86	0.00
S.Casilla H, 1	1	0	0	0	0	0	10	0.00
Romo S, 1-1	1	0	0	0	0	1	11	0.00

Fister pitched to 1 batter in the 7th. **Inherited runners-scored**—Smyly 1-1, Dotel 2-1, Coke 2-0. **IBB**—off Smyly (Sandoval). **HBP**—by Bumgarner (Fielder). **Umpires**—Home, Dan Iassogna; First, Fieldin Culbreth; Second, Brian O'Nora; Third, Brian Gorman; Right, Gerry Davis; Left, Joe West. **Time**—3:05. **Attendance**—42,982 (41,915).

WORLD SERIES GAME 3

ON BRINK OF GLORY

BY HENRY SCHULMAN

Ryan Vogelsong had lived, played and sweated his entire life for that one moment on a cold Saturday evening: bases loaded, two outs, a two-run lead and baseball's current King Kong at the plate. There was no way Bruce Bochy was going to deprive Vogelsong of the challenge, no way the pitcher was going to duck it.

"It's my first World Series," Vogelsong said. "I've been waiting for this since I was 5 years old, and I wasn't going to go down without a fight. That's for sure."

Vogelsong threw a two-seam fastball, Miguel Cabrera popped it up, the Giants survived their last real sweaty-palm moment and they beat the Tigers 2-0 at Comerica Park.

Now, there is no way the Giants can lose the 2012 World Series without a historic collapse. Twenty-three teams have taken a lead of three games to none, and all 23 have hoisted the trophy.

They have four shots to seal their second championship in three seasons, starting Sunday night with Matt Cain on the mound hoping to guide the Giants to a sweep that would allow them to tell Willie Mays, "We know how you feel."

Mays' 1954 New York Giants swept the Indians.

The Giants are as confident as they should be, given how they are dominating this Series, yet mindful that historic comebacks can happen.

After all, the Giants got here by winning two series they already "lost."

"It's very uplifting for us to take the first game here at their park," Sergio Romo said after saving a

Above: The Giants celebrate after the end of the game as they take a 3-0 lead in the World Series. The Giants won the game 2-0. *Carlos Avila Gonzalez*

Following Page: Giants' pitcher Ryan Vogelsong throws in the 1st inning during Game 3 of the World Series at Comerica Park. *Michael Macor*

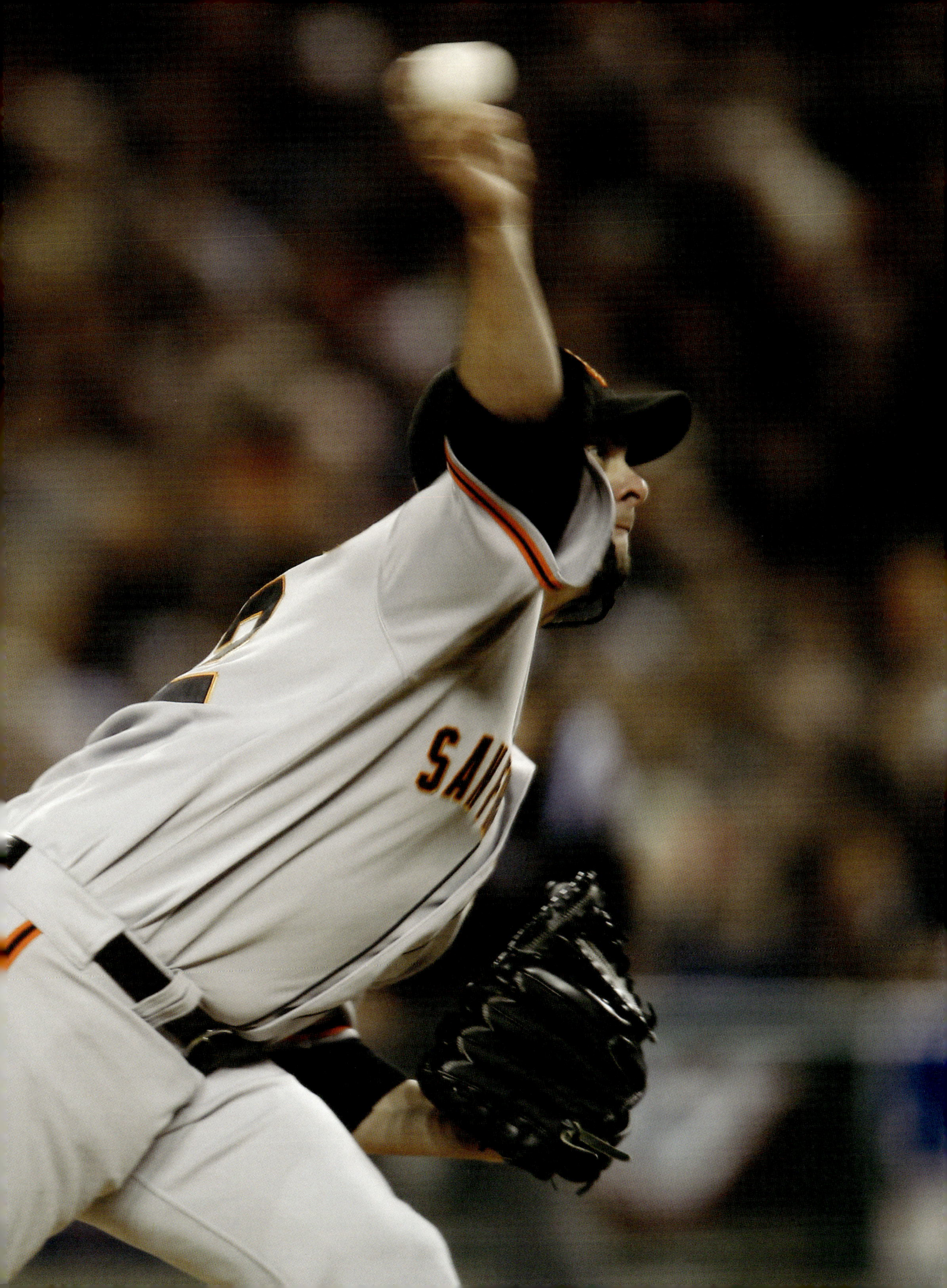

WORLD SERIES GAME 3

Above: Tigers' third baseman Miguel Cabrera is out at second base on a double play during the World Series Game 3. *Carlos Avila Gonzalez*

second consecutive 2-0 win.

"It's huge for us. We're up 3-0. They've got to beat us four times in a row. Do I like our chances? Of course. But anything's possible. Sleep on these guys? No chance."

Anything's possible? How about back-to-back World Series shutouts?

The Giants became the first team to accomplish that since the 1966 Orioles against the Dodgers. In the Giants' last back-to-back shutouts in one postseason, Ferdie Schupp and Rube Benton took it to Shoeless Joe Jackson's 1917 White Sox.

The feat is more impressive against a Detroit team that was whitewashed twice in the 2012 regular season.

The Giants used a familiar but unforeseen blue-

Above: Sergio Romo and Buster Posey hug as the Giants celebrate after the end of the game as they take a 3-0 lead in the World Series. *Carlos Avila Gonzalez*

WORLD SERIES: GAME 3   119

WORLD SERIES GAME 3

Above: Giants fans celebrate the first run of the game in the second inning during Game 3 of the World Series at Comerica Park in Detroit. *Lance Iversen*

print. Vogelsong pitched 5 2/3 innings and watched Tim Lincecum, who calls himself the Giants' "safety net," carry the shutout into the ninth.

The Giants got their runs in the second inning when burgeoning Series star Gregor Blanco hit an RBI triple off Anibal Sanchez to cash in Hunter Pence's leadoff walk and Brandon Crawford drove Blanco home with a two-out single.

The two RBI men also flashed their gloves at opportune moments. Crawford robbed Cabrera with a diving stop to get Lincecum the first out of the eighth. Blanco ran a long way into the left-field corner to snag Jhonny Peralta's long foul to start the ninth.

"I think that's a big out," Blanco said. "Always in the ninth to get the first out is huge. We were able to

SAN FRANCISCO GIANTS: A RETURN TO THE PINNACLE

do it and I think it helped Romo to finish it."

Romo might have lacked a lead, too, had Vogelsong not won his pivotal encounter in the fifth.

The Tigers loaded the bases with one out on singles by Alex Avila and Omar Infante and a walk to Austin Jackson. Vogelsong struck out Quintin Berry to bring up Cabrera, the first Triple Crown winner in 45 years and a terror with runners in scoring position.

Lincecum was ready in the bullpen, but Bochy did not rise from his seat.

"He's my guy," Bochy said of Vogelsong. "He's done it all year, keeping his poise, getting out of jams. He still had good stuff. I wasn't even thinking about getting him out."

And Vogelsong was not even thinking about trying to fool Cabrera. He threw two fastballs. Cabrera hit the first one foul. He hit the second in the air to Crawford, and the Giants exhaled.

"Right now, he's the best hitter in the game," Vogelsong said. "It's a lot easier to face him when there are two outs. I was just trying to make a pitch, and the way we were playing defense, I was really just trying to get him to put the ball in play somewhere because I had a good feeling we were going to catch it if he did."

Vogelsong is 3-0 with a 1.09 ERA, the lowest by any pitcher in a single postseason who has thrown at least 24 innings since Orel Hershiser's 1.05 during the Dodgers' 1988 championship run.

Lincecum has been just as impressive in relief – 13 innings, one run, 17 strikeouts.

"He's been throwing the ball great," Vogelsong said. "When the lights come on in the biggest stage, he's shown everybody what he's truly about."

Lincecum had a room full of reporters laughing when he said that once you win a title, "it's like that taste for that next ring is just sitting in your mouth the whole time. ... That sounds terrible.

"Let me rephrase that. It just leaves you wanting it even more."

He was right the first time. The Giants are so close to that ring they can taste it.

BOX SCORE

Giants 2, Tigers 0

Giants	AB	R	H	BI	BB	SO	Avg.
Pagan cf	4	0	0	0	0	1	.182
Scutaro 2b	4	0	0	0	0	1	.167
Sandoval 3b	4	0	2	0	0	0	.636
Arias 3b	0	0	0	0	0	0	—
Posey c	4	0	0	0	0	2	.273
Pence rf	3	1	2	0	1	0	.300
Belt 1b	4	0	0	0	0	3	.000
G.Blanco lf	4	1	1	1	0	1	.273
H.Sanchez dh	4	0	0	0	0	3	.000
B.Crawford ss	3	0	2	1	0	1	.222
Totals	**34**	**2**	**7**	**2**	**1**	**12**	
Detroit	AB	R	H	BI	BB	SO	Avg.
A.Jackson cf	2	0	1	0	2	0	.333
Berry lf	3	0	0	0	1	2	.000
Mi.Cabrera 3b	4	0	1	0	0	0	.222
Fielder 1b	4	0	0	0	0	2	.100
D.Young dh	3	0	0	0	1	0	.300
Dirks rf	3	0	0	0	1	1	.000
Jh.Peralta ss	4	0	0	0	0	0	.091
Avila c	4	0	1	0	0	1	.143
Infante 2b	4	0	2	0	0	1	.333
Totals	**31**	**0**	**5**	**0**	**5**	**7**	

Giants	020	000	000	—	2	7	1
Detroit	000	000	000	—	0	5	1

E—B.Crawford (1), A.Jackson (1). **LOB**—Giants 6, Detroit 9. **2B**—Sandoval (1). **3B**—G.Blanco (1). **RBIs**—G.Blanco (1), B.Crawford (1). **SB**—Pence (1), B.Crawford (1). **GIDP**—Berry, Fielder. **DP**—Giants 2 (Scutaro, B.Crawford, Belt), (Scutaro, B.Crawford, Belt).

Giants	IP	H	R	ER	BB	SO	NP	ERA
Vogelsong W, 1-0	5 2/3	5	0	0	4	3	104	0.00
Lincecum H, 1	2 1/3	0	0	0	1	3	32	0.00
Romo S, 2-2	1	0	0	0	0	1	17	0.00
Detroit	IP	H	R	ER	BB	SO	NP	ERA
A.Sanchez L, 0-1	7	6	2	2	1	8	117	2.57
Benoit	1	1	0	0	0	1	14	0.00
Coke	1	0	0	0	0	3	14	0.00

Inherited runners-scored—Lincecum 1-0. **WP**—A.Sanchez. **Umpires**—Home, Fieldin Culbreth; First, Brian O'Nora; Second, Brian Gorman; Third, Joe West; Right, Dan Iassogna; Left, Gerry Davis. **Time**—3:25. **Attendance**—42,262 (41,255).

WORLD SERIES GAME 4

TWICE IS NICE!

BY HENRY SCHULMAN

Matt Cain had one thought as he watched Marco Scutaro dig in for the at-bat of his life.

"I was just hoping he hadn't burned up all of his big hits through the year already," Cain said. "He's had so many. I was hoping he had another one in there for us."

The little Giant, the one they call "Blockbuster," did indeed. With two outs in the 10th inning, Scutaro floated a single to short center field. Austin Jackson charged hard but finally had to concede he would lose the battle with gravity.

The ball fell in, Ryan Theriot scored from second base, and three Sergio Romo strikeouts later,

Above: Giants' right fielder Hunter Pence is greeted in the dugout after scoring in the second inning on a Brandon Belt triple during Game 4 of the World Series in Detroit. *Michael Macor*

Above: Giants' second baseman Ryan Theriot scores on a Marco Scutaro single in the 10th inning during the World Series Game 4 at Comerica Park. *Carlos Alvia Gonzalez*

the San Francisco Giants were 2012 World Series champions after a 4-3 victory and a four game sweep of the Tigers that sounds as implausible as the comebacks against the Reds and Cardinals that made Sunday night's celebration possible.

When Romo threw a fastball past Miguel Cabrera for strike three, out three, the Giants charged toward one another on a frigid, damp field and set off the biggest celebration in San Francisco in, what, two years?

Romo pumped his fist three times as Buster Posey raced to hug him. They had won their second rings. Angel Pagan won his first and dropped to his knees in center field. In the mad scrum behind the mound, Scutaro hit Javier Lopez's mouth with the back of his head and drew blood, though the reliever did not mind.

"It's championship blood," Lopez said.

In the middle of the clubhouse, manager Bruce Bochy hoisted the Commissioner's Trophy over his

WORLD SERIES: GAME 4

WORLD SERIES GAME 4

Above: Giants Sergio Romo center and his teammates celebrate their World Series win over the Detroit Tigers at Comerica Park in Detroit. *Lance Iversen*

head and got a Champagne bath that drenched his big old dome.

He still looked stunned a half-hour later as he prepared to walk onto the field to do an interview.

"It's unbelievable what happened here the last two to three weeks," Bochy said. "I'm amazed. I couldn't be prouder of these guys."

To win one World Series in this era of parity and expanded playoffs is hard. Two in three years bespeaks a continuity of success rarely achieved.

The Giants are the second team to accomplish the feat since the playoff field was doubled from four to eight teams in 1995. The other was the New York Yankees, who won three in a row from 1998 to 2000. The Giants, Yankees, Marlins, Cardinals and Red Sox have won multiple titles in the wild-card era.

The Giants also got hot at the right time, as many title teams do. They finished their run to the championship with seven straight wins. Their longest winning streak during the regular season was six.

And a group of players who spoke so often about "team" put their final rally where their mouths were.

Theriot scored the winning run on a hit by the man who took his job, Scutaro, after the Giants acquired the 36-year-old from Colorado in July.

Theriot, the designated hitter, opened the 10th inning with a single off lefty Phil Coke, his only hit of the Series and third of the postseason. Brandon Crawford sacrificed and Pagan struck out to bring Scutaro to the plate with two outs.

Scutaro was a godsend for the Giants down the stretch, the MVP of the National League Championship Series. But to that point, he had been 3-for-15 in the World Series.

"My plan was to stay calm and just try to see the ball, just let it travel and try to make good contact," said Scutaro, who thought for a fleeting moment that Jackson would catch it.

"I thought, 'Get down! Don't stay up!'" he said. "When I saw it drop, I was thinking, 'Oh my God.'"

An entire visiting dugout and the faithful back home had the same thought as Theriot raced around third and scored easily ahead of a high throw. When Theriot rose from his slide, he ran just as hard toward the dugout, clapping his hands, with a deranged look.

"It was kind of a bitter-beer face," Brandon Belt said, laughing. "It was so awesome. Once again, Marco came through for us."

For the only time in the World Series, the Giants had a fight. The lead shifted from 1-0 Giants (on a Belt triple in the second) to 2-1 Tigers (on Cabrera's wind-blown home run against Cain in the third) to 3-2 Giants (on Posey's sixth inning home run, his first extra-base hit since his grand slam in NLCS Game 5 at Cincinnati).

Cain gave the lead back on a two-out, opposite-

WORLD SERIES: GAME 4

WORLD SERIES GAME 4

126 SAN FRANCISCO GIANTS: A RETURN TO THE PINNACLE

field homer by Delmon Young in the bottom of the sixth. Cain was angry that he let Detroit back into the game but said to himself, "You know what? It's over. I've got to get the next guy out, get us back
in the dugout and let these guys battle."

And they did. Jeremy Affeldt struck out Cabrera, Prince Fielder and Young in the eighth after a leadoff walk. Affeldt added a fourth straight strikeout in the ninth, which Santiago Casilla finished. Romo did what he has done all season, and all postseason, and saved it with no muss, no fuss — and in this case, no contact.

"We beat adversity, man. We did some stuff that's never been done before," Pagan said. "We came back twice in the playoffs. We refused to go home, and look where we are."

Opposite Page Top: The San Francisco Giants run to celebrate on the field after they defeated the Detroit Tigers in Game 4 of the World Series. The Giants are the 2012 World Champions after sweeping the Tigers. *Carlos Alvia Gonzalez*

Opposite Page Bottom: Tigers' left fielder Quintin Berry tossed his helmet after grounding out in the fifth inning during Game 4 of the World Series. *Michael Macor*

BOX SCORE

Giants 4, Tigers 3 (10)

Giants	AB	R	H	BI	BB	SO	Avg.
Pagan cf	5	0	0	0	0	2	.125
Scutaro 2b	4	1	2	1	1	0	.250
Sandoval 3b	5	0	1	0	0	2	.500
Arias 3b	0	0	0	0	0	0	—
Posey c	4	1	1	2	0	2	.267
Pence rf	4	1	1	0	0	3	.286
Belt 1b	3	0	1	1	1	1	.077
G.Blanco lf	4	0	1	0	0	2	.267
Theriot dh	4	1	1	0	0	1	.200
B.Crawford ss	3	0	1	0	0	0	.250
Totals	**36**	**4**	**9**	**4**	**2**	**13**	

Detroit	AB	R	H	BI	BB	SO	Avg.
A.Jackson cf	4	1	0	0	1	2	.231
Berry lf	3	0	0	0	0	0	.000
A.Garcia ph-rf	0	0	0	0	1	0	.000
D.Kelly ph	1	0	0	0	0	1	.000
Mi.Cabrera 3b	4	1	1	2	0	3	.231
Fielder 1b	4	0	0	0	0	2	.071
D.Young dh	4	1	2	1	0	2	.357
Dirks rf-lf	4	0	1	0	0	1	.111
Jh.Peralta ss	4	0	0	0	0	1	.067
Infante 2b	3	0	1	0	0	0	.333
Worth pr-2b	0	0	0	0	0	0	.000
G.Laird c	4	0	0	0	0	0	.000
Totals	**35**	**3**	**5**	**3**	**3**	**12**	

Giants	010	002	000	1	—	4	9	0
Detroit	002	001	000	0	—	3	5	0

LOB—Giants 5, Detroit 6. **2B**—Pence (1). **3B**—Belt (1). **HR**—Posey (1), off Scherzer; Mi.Cabrera (1), off M.Cain; D.Young (1), off M.Cain. **RBIs**—Scutaro (3), Posey 2 (3), Belt (1), Mi.Cabrera 2 (3), D.Young (1). **CS**—Belt (1). **S**—B.Crawford. **Runners moved up**—Theriot, Berry. **GIDP**—Sandoval. **DP**—Detroit 2 (G.Laird, G.Laird, Jh.Peralta), (Fielder, Jh.Peralta, Dotel).

Giants	IP	H	R	ER	BB	SO	NP	ERA
M.Cain	7	5	3	3	2	5	102	3.86
Affeldt	1 2/3	0	0	0	1	4	29	0.00
S.Casilla W, 1-0	1/3	0	0	0	0	0	5	0.00
Romo S, 3-3	1	0	0	0	0	3	15	0.00

Detroit	IP	H	R	ER	BB	SO	NP	ERA
Scherzer	6 1/3	7	3	3	1	8	90	4.26
Smyly	1/3	0	0	0	0	0	5	5.40
Dotel	1 1/3	0	0	0	1	1	18	0.00
Coke L, 0-1	2	2	1	1	0	4	27	2.70

Inherited runners-scored—Smyly 1-0, Dotel 1-0. **HBP**—by S.Casilla (Infante). **Umpires**—Home, Brian O'Nora; First, Brian Gorman; Second, Joe West; Third, Gerry Davis; Right, Fieldin Culbreth; Left, Dan Iassogna. **Time**—3:34. **Attendance**—42,152 (41,255).